MARY BERRY

COOK AND SHARE

BOOKS

CONTENTS

Introduction 7

Cook's Notes 13

———

FIRST COURSES 14

BRUNCH 36

SHARING 60

FISH 92

POULTRY 112

PORK, BEEF AND LAMB 136

VEGGIE MAINS 164

SALADS AND SIDES 192

BAKING 218

PUDDINGS AND DESSERTS 256

———

Conversion Chart 288

Recipe Finder by Style 290

Index 294

Thank Yous 302

INTRODUCTION

One of the great joys of cooking is sharing the results. Whether you are cooking for two people or for a gathering of friends and family, sharing is above all what life is about. And there's no better way to share than with homemade fresh food. It's a way to treat those close to you and to make people feel special. Sharing life, lessons and food has always been important to me. And as my family has grown and now that my grandchildren are young adults who are more creative with their food and have more adventurous tastes, my food has evolved and changed, too.

As it is a book about sharing, I've included Brunch and Sharing chapters for the first time to give a variety of recipes for informal gatherings – everyone together in the kitchen, passing the food around. Life is so much less formal nowadays, even for me and my husband. All my life I have loved the classic three-course dinner party, but we are doing structured parties less and less, and we are more keen on relaxed get togethers, often in the kitchen or outside when the weather is good. I do hope you find some inspiration in these pages for a gathering of your own. I've included a photo of every single recipe, which is so helpful and will give you an idea how to serve the recipes.

Nowadays, there is so much choice when it comes to kitchen equipment. All ovens are different and there are so many to choose from, whether gas or electric, single or double, fan assisted etc. Some ovens take a long time to heat up, while others are hot in no time. It is so important to make sure that the very first thing you do is preheat the oven, especially with baking, as cooking at an accurate temperature is imperative. A slight change in temperature will affect the look, rise and texture of a bake. In your oven a brownie may take a slightly different time to bake than in our oven, so make a note in your cookery book of any difference in the timings, so you know for next time. I love a recipe book that has handwriting in it – or use sticky notes. At home where we test the recipes, I have a very normal under-the-counter, fan-assisted double oven. It is a moderate oven that is the most popular nationally – no fancy ovens or equipment here! My recipes are for you to cook at home, so I make sure that we test everything with the equipment you would have. I talk to suppliers to find out what the bestselling equipment is and what type of food is the most popular. I want to use new ingredients and the old classics, so I can always (hopefully) give you a book with recipes you'll love to cook as a home cook. I leave the fancy food and equipment to the chefs, who I admire greatly.

I feel that many home cooks get stressed in the kitchen, so be kind to yourself and give yourself time. Once I have decided what to cook for a simple supper or special meal, the pressure is off – deciding what to cook is the big decision! When it comes to following recipes, I always say read the recipe at least twice before you start. Concentrate on each step of the recipe, from the ingredients list to checking which dishes or tins are used. And go through the method carefully, checking that you have everything you need. There's no sense in starting the recipe if you have the wrong size tin! And check if you need to marinate any of the ingredients ahead, or whether there's something simple you need to do, like removing butter from the fridge so it is easier to mix. It really does help if you take your time to read the recipe through carefully. Then, when you come to cook the dish, you'll know you are all set up and there will be no surprises. When you open the cupboard for five spice powder, for example, you won't discover that there isn't any! But, equally, before you start shopping for a recipe, check you don't have three jars of five spice powder in the cupboard already!

Although, saying that, swapping ingredients is ok sometimes! If you are making a casserole and the recipe calls for white onions and you only have red, that would be a good swap. And switching root vegetables can work, too. This way, you can add your own stamp on a recipe. But don't swap too much or the recipe may not work! This is another occasion when making notes in your cookery book will help; if you've tried a variation to a recipe, write it down and remind yourself of the success – or not – for next time.

So, I hope you enjoy this new book, *Cook and Share*. Take time to cook, share and enjoy the dishes and enjoy yourselves! Share a moment with friends over a cup of tea and a white chocolate shortbread biscuit (see page 252), a coffee and a stack of pancakes at brunch (see page 47), a glass of wine and a plate of warming Beef Bourguignon Pie (see page 153) or simply a slice of Sunday Lunch Plum Crumble Cake (see page 281). However it comes about, spend time with the people close to you and you may even get some recipes shared with you in return!

Mary Berry

KITCHEN SUPPERS

Chicken Spinach and
Tomato Lasagne

Sunrise Fruit Salad

———

Shepherd's Puff Pastry Pie

Limoncello Passion Panna Cotta

———

Smoked Haddock and Celeriac
and Potato Mash Fish Pie

Chocolate and Brandy Shots

SPECIAL OCCASION
DINNERS

Smoked Salmon and
Watercress Paté

Roast Rack of Lamb
with Celeriac Purée

Glazed French Peach Tart

———

Tuna Ceviche with Pickled
Ginger and Salsa

Fillet Steak for Two with Green
Peppercorn and Brandy Sauce

Glorious Chocolate Truffle Dessert

———

Scallops with Garlic King Oyster
Mushrooms and Tarragon

Miso Salmon with
Aromatic Spinach

Feathered White Chocolate
Cheesecake

PICNIC SPREAD

Tear and Share Cheese
and Herb Rolls

Red Pepper, Cheese and
Chive Canapé Tarts

Jumbo Sausage Rolls

Jumbo Lentil Rolls

Provence Tomato and
Garlic Pistou Tart

Hot-smoked Salmon Rice
and Asparagus Salad

Coronation Coleslaw

Greek Salad with Asparagus

Lemon and Passion Fruit Traybake

The Ultimate Chocolate Brownies

Banana Fruit Bread

BEST BRUNCH

Smashed Avocado, Asparagus
and Fried Egg on Sourdough

American-style Pancakes with
Bacon and Maple Syrup

Match Day Hot Dogs

Fruit Kebabs with Lemon Dip

Ginger and Orange Polenta Cake

GARDENER'S SHOWSTOPPERS

Autumn Leek and Mushroom Soup

Gardener's Stuffed Squash

Five Veg Pasta

Forest Bean Salad with
Herb Lemon Dressing

Harissa Roasted
Chanternay Carrots

Hispi Cabbage Noisette

Leek and Potato Gratin

Garlic Roasted Potatoes
with Rosemary

Roasted Tomato and Basil Soup

Spaghetti with Peas and Pesto

Spiced Apple Strudel

Sunday Lunch Plum Crumble Cake

Windfall Pie

Winter Parsnip and Chestnut Soup

TAKEAWAY NIGHT IN

Thai Green Curry

Vegetable Pad Thai

Curried Squash and
Paneer Filo Samosas

Sabzi Vegetable Curry

Black Bean Beef Noodle Stir-fry

Prawn Stir-fry with Ginger,
Coconut and Chilli

Halloumi and Sweet Potato Fries

SHARING BOARDS

Bresaola Sharing Board with
Rocket, Parmesan and Bean Salad

Coriander Roasted Vegetables
with Basil Olive Dip

Smoked Salmon and
Burrata Sharing Platter

TEENAGERS COME ROUND

Eggy Bread Avocado
and Ham Sandwich

Match Day Hot Dogs

Halloumi and Sweet Potato
Fries with Chilli Dip

Chipchip Cassoulet

Sticky Short Beef Ribs
and Lemon Coleslaw

Smoked Haddock Macaroni Cheese

Trio of Skewers – Harissa
Halloumi and Squash, Black
Bean Chicken and Honey-
glazed Salmon and Courgette

Pair of Koftas – Minted Lamb
with Cucumber Dip and
Beef with Tomato Salsa

Jumbo Sausage and
Jumbo Lentil Rolls

Spicy Pork with Sweet Potato
and Black-eyed Beans

EATS FOR DRINKS

Salmon, Goat's Cheese
and Cucumber Canapé

Red Pepper, Cheese and
Chive Canapé Tarts

Herb Blinis

Spiced Beef with Chicory

Hoso Maki

Sushi Squares with Smoked
Salmon and Pickled Ginger

EASTER AND
CHRISTMAS TREATS

Sunday Best Minted
Lamb – for Easter

Simnel Cake – for Easter
or Mothering Sunday

———

Star Almond Mince Pies
– for Christmas time

Clementine Cake – for
Christmas time

Smoked Haddock and Celeriac
and Potato Mash Fish Pie
– for Christmas Eve

Avocado, Beetroot and Prawn
Stack – Christmas Day starter

Tiramisu Red Fruit Trifle –
Christmas Day pudding

FIVE SUNDAY LUNCHES

Two Roast Chickens
and Potato Gratin

Sunday Lunch Plum Crumble Cake

———

Sunday Best Minted Lamb

Windfall Pie

———

Loin of Stuffed Pork with
Crackling and White Wine Gravy

Spiced Apple Strudel

———

Beef Bourguignon Pie

Hazelnut Meringue Roulade

———

Salmon en Croûte with
Spinach and Dill

Baked Ricotta Cheesecake
with Blackberry Coulis

COOK'S NOTES

FREE-RANGE MEAT

Try to buy the best-quality meat that you can afford. British farmers have some of the highest food standards in the world and it really does make a difference. Animals should be looked after and loved, fed properly and regularly, and respected for the nourishment they provide. I always use free-range chicken and eggs, and would recommend that you do, too.

SUSTAINABLE FISH

As with free-range meat, try to buy fish that is sustainably sourced – this means it has been fished in a way that doesn't damage fish stocks and protects the habitat. It will advertise itself as such on the packet, or ask your fishmonger or at the fish counter in your local supermarket. The levels of fish stocks do change, so while I have tried to include fish that are on the sustainability list, do swap one for another if necessary.

LARGE EGGS

We use large eggs, unless otherwise stated.

METRIC AND IMPERIAL

I have provided both metric and imperial measurements. When you are following a recipe, it's best to stick to one or the other – particularly if you are baking. (See the Conversion Table on pages 288–9.) Spoon measurements are level, unless otherwise stated.

OVEN AND GRILL TEMPERATURES

As ovens and grills vary in the amount of heat they produce, you may need to cook a dish for slightly longer or shorter than the recipe stipulates, depending on your appliance.

SCALES AND MEASURING SPOONS

I find digital scales really are the best and the most accurate. I changed my thoughts on this latterly. Years ago, I swore by the spring balance scales because the digital ones available weren't accurate. Now, however, everything is so much more efficient and digital scales are definitely my first choice. Another essential kitchen item is a set of measuring spoons for measuring baking powder, spices and small amounts of liquids, such as soy sauce and olive oil. It's so important to get the same results every time.

OVENPROOF FRYING PANS AND FLAMEPROOF CASSEROLES

A number of the recipes for stews and one-pan dishes begin on the hob and end up in the oven. I tend to use large, deep frying pans, as the ones I have at home are ovenproof, but it would be just as good to use a flameproof casserole. So long as it has a lid that fits and is suitable to use on the hob and in the oven, it will do the job.

FIRST COURSES

SALMON, GOAT'S CHEESE AND CUCUMBER CANAPÉ

This scrumptious cold canapé is quick and easy and will be popular. Rolled like little cigars, you can use smoked salmon, smoked trout slices or even gravadlax. Best to choose long thin slices, rather than slices with straggly edges.

MAKES 15–18

¼ cucumber

120g (4¼oz) smoked
  salmon (cocktail slices,
  if possible – see page 20)

75g (3oz) soft goat's
  cheese in a tub

½ bunch of dill, chopped

½ lemon

Mary's Tips

* *Can be made up to
4 hours ahead.*

* *Not suitable for freezing.*

Cut the cucumber in half lengthways. Scoop out the seeds with a teaspoon, then slice lengthways into small matchstick shapes about 4cm (1½in) long.

Place the salmon slices on a board. Trim them to roughly 8 × 3cm (3¼ × 1¼in). You should have around 15–18 slices. Spread each slice with a little soft goat's cheese and season with freshly ground black pepper.

Sprinkle chopped dill over one narrow end of each strip. Place two matchsticks of cucumber on top. Roll up each slice into a cigar shape.

Arrange the canapés neatly on a small platter. Squeeze lemon juice over the tops and sprinkle with a little black pepper just before serving.

RED PEPPER, CHEESE AND CHIVE CANAPÉ TARTS

These are substantial canapés. Perfect for a hungry crowd.
Use deep mini muffin tins but tins can vary in size slightly,
so if your tin is shallow, you may make more tarts.

MAKES 24

CHEESE PASTRY

150g (5oz) plain flour, plus a little extra for dusting

75g (3oz) cold butter, cubed

30g (1oz) Parmesan, grated

A pinch of paprika

About ½ egg, beaten (approx. 2–3 tbsp)

FILLING

115g (4oz) chargrilled red peppers in oil from a jar, drained and chopped

1 garlic clove, crushed

1 tbsp sun-dried tomato paste

75g (3oz) mature Cheddar, grated

1 large egg

75ml (2½fl oz) pouring double cream

2 tbsp chopped chives

8 cherry tomatoes, each sliced into 3

Mary's Tips

* *It's worth taking the time to grease the tins well, to ease removal of the cooked tarts.*

You will need two 12-hole deep mini muffin tins, well greased, and a 6cm (2½in) round cutter.

To make the pastry, measure the flour, butter, Parmesan and paprika into a food processor. Whiz until breadcrumb stage. Add the beaten egg and whiz again until the dough just comes together. Tip out on to a floured work surface and gently knead into a ball. Using a rolling pin, roll the pastry out very thinly and stamp out 24 rounds using the round cutter. Line the mini muffin tins and prick the bases with a fork. Chill in the freezer for 20 minutes.

Preheat the oven to 200°C/180°C Fan/Gas 6.

Place the peppers in a bowl. Stir in the garlic and sun-dried tomato paste. Mix and season with salt and freshly ground black pepper. Divide between the muffin tins and place a small pile of cheese on top of each one.

Crack the egg into a jug, pour in the cream, add the chives and season. Mix until combined, then carefully pour or spoon into the tins over the filling. Top each tart with a slice of tomato and bake in the preheated oven for about 18 minutes, or until pale golden brown and set in the middle.

Serve warm.

SMOKED SALMON AND WATERCRESS PATÉ

Made in a loaf tin, this paté is easy to slice and looks good on the plate. Cocktail strips of smoked salmon (long strips) are not always available. If you can't find them, use regular sliced smoked salmon and patch it over the tin. It helps if the terrine is really cold before slicing, so pop it in the freezer for half an hour.

SERVES 8–10

Small bunch of dill, 4 small sprigs reserved and the remainder chopped

115g (4oz) butter, softened, plus extra for buttering the dish and for the salmon

150g (5oz) fresh salmon fillet, skinned

350g (12oz) smoked salmon (cocktail slices, if possible)

2 tsp hot horseradish sauce

180g (6½oz) full-fat cream cheese

1 tbsp fresh lemon juice

Small bunch of watercress, roughly chopped, plus sprigs to serve

Preheat the oven to 180°C/160°C Fan/Gas 4 and butter the inside of a 450g (1lb) loaf tin.

Cut a piece of non-stick baking paper and line the base and long sides of the tin (the ends do not need lining). Leave the lining paper hanging over the edge – this will help you remove the finished paté. Lay 3 reserved sprigs of dill in the centre of the base of the tin.

Place a piece on foil on the worktop and butter the centre. Sit the salmon fillet on the buttered foil, spread a little more butter on top and season with salt and freshly ground black pepper. Place the remaining reserved sprig of dill on top, then fold the foil into a parcel and place on a baking sheet. Bake in the preheated oven for about 15 minutes, or until just cooked. Leave to cool in the foil.

Line the prepared loaf tin with strips of smoked salmon along the base and sides, overlapping each slice, to leave no gaps. Let some of the salmon overhang the edge of the tin.

Place the remaining smoked salmon into a food processor (you should have 60–70g/2¼–2½oz). Add the cold cooked salmon fillet, the horseradish, cream cheese, soft butter, lemon juice and a little salt and plenty of freshly ground pepper. Whiz until smooth.

recipe continues overleaf...

Place 3 spoonfuls of salmon paté into a bowl for the centre layer, add the chopped watercress and dill, and mix well. Check the seasoning and set aside.

Spread half of the paté from the mixer into the base of the tin and level the surface.

Spread the watercress mixture over the top and use the back of a spoon to push it into the edges and corners in an even layer.

Spread the remaining salmon paté over the watercress layer and level with the back of a spoon.

Flip the excess smoked salmon slices over the top and press down firmly. Cover and chill for at least 5 hours, until firm.

Serve one thick slice per person with extra sprigs of watercress on the side.

HERB BLINIS

These are a brilliant nibble to have ready when friends come round. The batter can be made a day ahead and the various toppings can be placed on top up to 1 hour ahead.

MAKES 48

115g (4oz) self-raising flour
½ tsp bicarbonate of soda
2 eggs
75ml (2½fl oz) milk
2 tbsp chopped chives
1 tbsp oil, plus extra
   as needed

Mary's Tips

* *The batter can be made a day in advance. No need to refrigerate, as being room temperature will allow it to breathe.*
* *Blinis can be made up to 6 hours ahead and freeze well without topping. Decorate up to 1 hour ahead and store in the fridge.*
* *The toppings can be prepared in advance and stored in the fridge.*

Measure the flour and bicarb into a bowl and make a well in the centre. Break the eggs into the centre and gradually pour in the milk, whisking all the time with a hand whisk. Stir in the chives, season with salt and freshly ground black pepper, and stir to make a smooth batter.

Heat the oil in a large frying pan over a high heat. When hot, spoon teaspoonfuls of mixture into the pan to make approximately 5cm (2in) circles. Reduce the heat to medium and fry for 1–2 minutes, until lightly brown, then turn over and fry on the other side until lightly brown too. You will know when the blinis are ready to turn over as little bubbles appear.

Repeat with the rest of the batter, adding a little more oil, if required, and frying in batches.

Transfer the cooked blinis to a plate lined with kitchen paper to absorb any excess oil, then leave to cool on a wire rack until cold. Cover until ready to use.

Add toppings to serve (see page 24).

PEA AND FETA BLINIS

MAKES 16

115g (4oz) frozen
  petits pois
1 banana shallot,
  finely chopped
1 tbsp mayonnaise
55g (2oz) feta, crumbled
2–3 small radishes, each
  cut into thin slices

Bring a saucepan of water to the boil and cook the peas and shallot for 2–3 minutes, until just cooked and softened. Drain and refresh in cold water, then tip into a bowl.

Add the mayonnaise, season with salt and freshly ground black pepper and mash with a fork or whiz with a hand blender, until you have a chunky purée.

Spoon a little of the purée on each blini, then top with some feta and a thin slice of radish.

GINGER AND CHILLI PRAWN BLINIS

MAKES 16

1–2 tbsp sweet chilli sauce
½ tsp finely grated
  fresh root ginger
16 king prawns, peeled
90g (3½oz) full-fat
  cream cheese
1 tbsp chopped chives

Mix the sweet chilli sauce and ginger in a bowl. Add the prawns and season with a little salt and freshly ground black pepper.

Spread a little cream cheese on each blini, top with a prawn and sprinkle with some chopped chives.

AVOCADO, OLIVE AND TOMATO BLINIS

MAKES 16

1 ripe avocado, peeled
  and cut into chunks
2 tbsp fresh lemon juice
8 small cherry
  tomatoes, halved
8 pitted black
  olives, halved

Tip the avocado into a bowl and mash with a fork to make a fairly smooth purée. Season with salt and freshly ground black pepper and add the lemon juice. Mix well.

Spoon some avocado mixture on each blini, then top with a tomato half and an olive half.

AVOCADO, BEETROOT
AND PRAWN STACK

*This is a perfect dinner party first course. It can be made ahead and,
as it's served cold, it can be ready with no last-minute preparation.
If you only have hot horseradish, use just one teaspoon.*

MAKES 6

300g (10½oz) cooked
  beetroot, peeled
  and finely diced

1 tbsp balsamic glaze

2 ripe avocados, peeled
  and finely diced

Juice of ½ lemon

½ bunch of dill, chopped,
  plus extra to garnish

1 tbsp mayonnaise

1 tbsp full-fat
  crème fraîche

1 tbsp creamed
  horseradish sauce

¼ small cucumber,
  peeled, deseeded
  and finely diced

350g (12oz) small cooked
  and shelled prawns,
  dried on kitchen paper

Mary's Tips

* Can be assembled up to
  2 hours ahead and kept in
  the fridge. Keep the ring
  on until ready to plate up.

* Not suitable for freezing.

* If you don't have 7cm
  cooking rings, assemble
  the stacks in glasses or
  glass ramekins so that
  the layers are visible.

You will need six 7cm (2¾in) cooking rings about 5cm
(2in) deep. Place them on a baking sheet lined with
non-stick baking paper.

Place the beetroot and balsamic glaze into a small
bowl. Season with salt and freshly ground black
pepper and mix well.

Place the avocado, lemon juice and dill into another
small bowl. Lightly mash some of the avocado with
a fork to help it to hold together, leaving some diced
pieces to give texture. Mix well and season.

Measure the mayonnaise, crème fraîche and
horseradish into a third small bowl. Season, then stir
in the prawns and cucumber. Mix well.

Spoon the beetroot into the bases of the cooking
rings. Press down using the back of a teaspoon.
Divide the avocado between the rings and smooth
with the back of a teaspoon to cover the beetroot.
Finally, top with the prawns and gently press down
to smooth the surface. Chill for at least 30 minutes.

To serve, slide a fish slice under the ring and sit it
on a small plate. Remove the ring and garnish with a
sprig of dill. Repeat with the remaining rings. Serve
with Tear and Share Cheese and Herb Rolls (see page
255) or brown bread and butter.

SUMMER SOUP –
PEA, POTATO AND BASIL

Bursting with summer flavours, this soup can be made from homegrown veg, if you grow your own. I like texture in my soup, which is why I remove some of the vegetables to add after blending.

SERVES 6

A knob of butter

2 tbsp sunflower oil

2 onions, finely chopped

2 garlic cloves, crushed

200g (7oz) potatoes, peeled

150g (5oz) fresh broad beans, removed from their pods (podded weight)

750ml (1⅓ pints) hot chicken or vegetable stock

225g (8oz) fresh peas or frozen petits pois

175g (6oz) broccoli, cut into bite-sized florets

½ bunch of basil, roughly torn

3 tbsp pouring double cream

Mary's Tips

* *Best made on the day to keep the bright colour.*

* *Not suitable for freezing as it will lose its colour.*

Heat the butter and oil in a large saucepan over a medium-high heat. Add the onions and garlic and fry for 5 minutes.

Stir in the potatoes and fry for 3–4 minutes.

Add the broad beans and stock, and season with salt and freshly ground black pepper. Cover, reduce the heat and simmer for about 15 minutes.

Add the peas and broccoli and boil over a high heat for 5 minutes, or until the broccoli is tender. Scoop out 5 large spoonfuls of vegetables into a bowl and set aside. Add the basil to the pan and whiz with a hand blender until smooth.

Check the seasoning and serve hot with the reserved cooked vegetables stirred through and the cream drizzled over the top.

AUTUMN LEEK AND MUSHROOM SOUP

Perfect for using leeks in season and very welcoming on chilly days. Soup is the perfect sharing recipe – one pan and two bowls, sharing with a friend for a natter and a catch up.

SERVES 6

1 tbsp sunflower oil

A knob of butter

3 medium leeks, trimmed and sliced

350g (12oz) white closed-cup mushrooms, roughly chopped

2 large potatoes (300–350g/10½–12oz each), peeled and diced

750ml (1⅓ pints) hot chicken or vegetable stock

4 tbsp pouring double cream

1–2 tbsp finely chopped tarragon

Mary's Tips

* *Can be made up to 2 days ahead. Chill and store in the fridge.*

* *Freezes well.*

Heat the oil and butter in a large saucepan over a high heat. Add the leeks and mushrooms and fry for about 5 minutes, stirring occasionally.

Stir in the potato and pour in the stock. Season with salt and freshly ground pepper. Bring up to the boil, then cover, reduce the heat and simmer gently for about 15 minutes, or until the potatoes are tender.

Remove from the heat and allow to cool slightly, then whiz with a hand blender or food processor until smooth.

Check the seasoning and ladle into warm bowls to serve. Add a swirl of cream and a sprinkling of tarragon to each bowl.

WINTER PARSNIP AND CHESTNUT SOUP WITH CARAMELISED CHESTNUTS

Serve in small bowls as this soup is rich and creamy. The glazed chestnuts make it extra special. Frozen chestnuts are wonderful as they have the skin removed, so are ready to use. If frozen chestnuts are not available, use vacuum-packed cooked ones instead.

SERVES 6

2 tbsp olive or sunflower oil

2 medium leeks, trimmed and thinly sliced

2 celery sticks, trimmed and sliced

500g (1lb 2oz) parsnips, peeled and cut into 2cm (¾in) cubes

250g (9oz) frozen chestnuts, thawed and halved

1.2 litres (2 pints) hot chicken or vegetable stock

3 tbsp full-fat crème fraîche

GARNISH

A knob of butter

115g (4oz) frozen chestnuts, thawed and thinly sliced

1 tsp runny honey

Mary's Tip

* *The soup freezes well.*

Heat the oil in a large saucepan over a medium-high heat. Add the leeks and celery and fry for a few minutes until they start to soften. Add the parsnips and chestnuts and cook for about 5 minutes, stirring occasionally.

Pour in the stock and season with salt and freshly ground black pepper. Cover and bring up to the boil. Lower the heat and simmer for about 20 minutes, until the parsnips are tender.

Remove from the heat and whiz with a hand blender or food processor. Add the crème fraîche and whiz again. Check the seasoning.

Meanwhile, for the garnish, melt the butter in a small frying pan over a high heat. When foaming, add the chestnuts and honey and stir to coat evenly. Fry for a few minutes, until the chestnuts are golden and caramelised.

Ladle the soup into warm bowls and sprinkle the chestnuts on top to serve.

ROASTED TOMATO AND BASIL SOUP

Such a favourite with all the family, I've kept this recipe simple but by roasting the tomatoes first you get the best flavour.

SERVES 6

1.5kg (3lb 5oz) large ripe tomatoes, halved

3 tbsp olive oil

1 tbsp balsamic vinegar

1 large onion, chopped

2 large garlic cloves, crushed

2 tbsp tomato purée

½ bunch of basil, chopped, with some leaves reserved to garnish

1 tsp caster sugar

150ml (¼ pint) hot chicken or vegetable stock

Cheddar, grated, to garnish

Mary's Tips

* *Can be made up to 2 days ahead. Chill and store in the fridge.*

* *Freezes for up to a month.*

* *It is easy to skin the tomatoes if they are roasted on the tray with the cut side down – the skin can then be 'pinched off' with the thumb and forefinger.*

Preheat the oven to 200°C/180°C Fan/Gas 6.

Place the tomatoes skin side up in a single layer in a large roasting tin. Drizzle with 2 tablespoons of the oil and the balsamic vinegar, and season with salt and freshly ground black pepper. Roast in the oven for about 30 minutes, until soft and the skins are shrivelled. Leave to cool slightly then slip the flesh out of the skins. Discard the skins.

Heat the remaining oil in a large saucepan over a medium-high heat. Add the onion and garlic and fry for 5 minutes, stirring occasionally.

Add the tomato flesh, all the juices from the roasting tin and the tomato purée, and stir. Cover and bring up to the boil. Reduce the heat and simmer for 10 minutes, until the onions are soft.

Add the basil and sugar and whiz with a hand blender until completely smooth. Stir in the stock, check the seasoning and whiz again until smooth.

Serve hot, sprinkled with grated cheese and a few basil leaves and alongside some crusty bread.

BRUNCH

BACON AND EGG
BREAKFAST CROUSTADES

All the breakfast favourites in a croustade – it's like a tart but has a bread base.

MAKES 4

4 slices white bread

30g (1oz) butter, melted

3 rashers of unsmoked back bacon, rind removed, cut into small pieces

75g (3oz) button mushrooms, sliced

55g (2oz) mature Cheddar, grated

4 tbsp pouring double cream

4 small or medium eggs

Mary's Tips

* *The croustade base can be cooked up to 2 hours ahead. Complete to serve.*
* *Not suitable for freezing.*
* *Don't waste the leftover bread. Whiz it up in a processor to make fresh breadcrumbs (they freeze well) or cut into cubes and fry to make croûtons.*

Preheat the oven to 220°C/200°C Fan/Gas 7. You will need a 4-hole Yorkshire pudding tin and a 12.5cm (5in) round cutter.

Place the slices of bread on a board. Using a rolling pin, roll each slice out thinly. Stamp out one round from each slice using the cutter and brush both sides with butter. Brush the 4-hole tin with butter then line with the bread. Bake in the preheated oven for about 10–12 minutes, until golden and crisp.

Meanwhile, place the bacon pieces in a small frying pan over a medium heat. Fry for 2–3 minutes, until the bacon is starting to brown.

Add the mushrooms and fry for another 2–3 minutes, until the mushrooms are soft, cooked and dry.

Divide the bacon and mushroom mixture between the cooked bread slices, then divide the cheese and double cream between them. Season with salt and freshly ground black pepper. Return to the oven for 5 minutes.

Remove the tin from the oven and make a small well in the centre of each croustade with the back of a spoon. Crack an egg into each one and return to the oven for a final 8–10 minutes, or until the whites are set and the yolks are done to your liking.

Serve hot.

SHAKSHUKA

A popular Middle Eastern and North African dish, this can now be found on many breakfast menus. The name means 'mix up' in Arabic. It has a spiced tomato base with eggs on top and is such a quick and easy dish to make from store-cupboard ingredients. There are many variations and additions to this historic recipe; some add aubergine, feta or spicy sausage.

SERVES 4

2 tbsp olive or
  sunflower oil
2 onions, roughly chopped
2 garlic cloves, crushed
1 red chilli, deseeded
  and finely diced
2 × 400g tins chopped
  tomatoes
1 heaped tbsp sun-
  dried tomato paste
Scant tsp caster sugar
4 eggs
2 tbsp chopped
  flat-leaf parsley

Mary's Tips

* *The tomato base can be made up to 8 hours ahead. Heat before adding the eggs.*
* *Not suitable for freezing.*

You will need a deep frying pan or sauté pan with a lid.

Heat the oil in a deep frying pan over a medium-high heat. Add the onions and fry for 5 minutes.

Add the garlic and chilli and fry for 30 seconds. Stir in the chopped tomatoes, sun-dried tomato paste and sugar and bring up to the boil. Reduce the heat and simmer gently, without a lid, for about 10 minutes, until the sauce has reduced and thickened and the onion is tender. Season well with salt and freshly ground black pepper.

Using the back of a spoon, make four dips in the sauce and carefully crack an egg into each one. Cover the pan with a lid and simmer on the hob over a gentle heat for about 6 minutes, or until the whites are set but the yolks are runny.

Sprinkle with the parsley and serve immediately from the pan with pitta or crusty bread.

FRITTATA WITH SPINACH, FETA AND TOMATOES

A wonderful brunch dish to feed the hungry. Change the cheese for mature Cheddar if you prefer.

SERVES 6–8

2 tbsp sunflower oil

1 small onion, thinly sliced

½ red pepper, deseeded and diced

1 large garlic clove, crushed

115g (4oz) baby spinach

8 large eggs

150g (5oz) feta, cut into small pieces

115g (4oz) cherry tomatoes, halved or quartered

Mary Tips

* Best made and served.
* Not suitable for freezing.

Preheat the oven to 200°C/180°C Fan/Gas 6. You will need a 26cm (10½in) non-stick ovenproof frying pan.

Heat the oil in the pan over a medium heat. Add the onion and pepper and fry gently for about 10 minutes, until the vegetables are tender, stirring occasionally.

Add the garlic and spinach and fry for 2–3 minutes, until wilted. Leave the vegetables in the pan.

Meanwhile, beat the eggs in a jug and season well with salt and freshly ground black pepper.

Pour into the pan and swirl around to coat the vegetables. Fry for 3–4 minutes, until the egg starts to set around the edges of the pan.

Scatter over the feta and tomatoes. Transfer to the oven for 10–15 minutes, until the egg is completely set in the middle and the frittata is lightly golden on top and underneath.

Slide on to a plate and slice into wedges to serve hot.

SMASHED AVOCADO, ASPARAGUS AND FRIED EGG ON SOURDOUGH

A romantic breakfast or brunch for two. Quick, easy and scrummy! To share breakfast is just as special as sharing supper – a great way to start the day.

SERVES 2

6 asparagus spears
1 ripe avocado, halved
A dash of fresh lemon juice
1 tbsp chopped flat-leaf parsley
2 tbsp sunflower oil
2 large eggs
2 slices sourdough or granary bread
1 tbsp mayonnaise
1 tsp dried chilli flakes

Mary's Tips

* Best made and served.
* Not suitable for freezing.
* Be careful not to overcook the asparagus – it should be al dente. These timings are for thick asparagus spears.

Remove the woody ends from the asparagus. Blanch the asparagus in a pan of boiling salted water for 3–4 minutes. Drain and refresh under cold water. Drain again and pat dry with kitchen paper.

Scoop the avocado into a bowl and mash with a fork. Add a little lemon juice and season well with salt and freshly ground black pepper. Stir in the parsley.

Heat the oil in a small frying pan over a high heat. Add the eggs and fry for 3–4 minutes, until the white is set but the yolk is runny.

Toast the bread and place on a board. Spread each slice with mayonnaise and top with the smashed avocado. Arrange three asparagus spears on top of each slice and sit a fried egg on top.

Sprinkle with chilli flakes and black pepper, and serve hot.

AMERICAN-STYLE PANCAKES WITH BACON AND MAPLE SYRUP

Hearty and filling, these pancakes are thicker than crepes, more like Scotch pancakes. A gang of teenagers will love this!

SERVES 4

12 rashers of streaky bacon
200g (7oz) plain flour
2 tsp baking powder
55g (2oz) caster sugar
3 large eggs, separated
200ml (⅓ pint) milk
Sunflower oil, for frying
Maple syrup, to serve

Mary's Tips

* Best made and served.
* Not suitable for freezing.

Preheat the grill to high and line the grill pan with foil.

Arrange the bacon in a single layer on the grill pan. Grill for 5–8 minutes, turning once, until the bacon is crispy. Place the bacon on kitchen paper to drain any excess fat, then keep warm while you make the pancakes.

Measure the flour, baking powder and sugar into a large mixing bowl. Make a well in the centre and add the egg yolks and a little of the milk. Whisk well to remove any lumps. Slowly pour in the remaining milk, whisking until you have a smooth batter.

Place the egg whites in a large bowl and whisk until stiff. Carefully fold them into the batter.

Heat a little oil in a large non-stick frying pan. Add 3–4 large tablespoonsful of the mixture to the pan and fry for 1–2 minutes, until bubbles appear on the surface. Flip over and cook on the other side until lightly golden. Repeat with the remaining mixture.

Serve the pancakes with the crispy bacon on top and drizzle with lots of maple syrup.

CINNAMON CREPES

So delicate and thin, these are often only served on pancake day, when in fact they are perfect for brunch or breakfast. The first pancake is always a little tricky and may stick. For a traditional crepe, leave out the cinnamon.

MAKES 10

115g (4oz) plain flour
1 tbsp ground cinnamon
2 eggs
225ml (8fl oz) milk
2 tbsp sunflower oil
2 lemons, cut into
    thin wedges
55g (2oz) caster sugar

Mary's Tips

* *Best made and
served – share the
cooking and eating.*

You will need a crepe pan or a non-stick 23cm (9in) shallow frying pan.

Measure the flour and cinnamon into a bowl. Crack the eggs into the bowl and add a dash of the milk. Whisk together using a balloon whisk to make a thick batter. Slowly pour in the remaining milk, whisking until a smooth thin batter.

Heat a little of the oil in a crepe pan or small non-stick frying pan. Pour just enough of the batter into the pan to give a large disc in the centre. Swirl the pan to make a thin pancake. Fry for a few minutes, until golden on the underside and set on top, then flip over and fry for 1–2 minutes on the other side. Tip on to a warm plate.

Continue with the remaining oil and batter and place a piece of kitchen paper or non-stick baking paper in between the pancakes to prevent sticking.

Serve the warm crepes with a squeeze of lemon and a sprinkling of sugar.

EGGY BREAD AVOCADO
AND HAM SANDWICH

Remember eggy bread? We used to eat it on its own, now we have an eggy bread sandwich. Choose your favourite pickle or chutney to go with this.

MAKES 2

4 slices granary bread

30g (1oz) butter, softened, plus extra for frying

2 tbsp pickle or chutney

½ ripe avocado, peeled and sliced

55g (2oz) mature Cheddar, grated

2 slices ham

2 eggs

A dash of sunflower oil, for frying

Mary's Tips

* Can be assembled up to 1 hour before. Dip in the beaten egg just before frying.

* Not suitable for freezing.

Place the bread on a board. Spread two slices with butter and the pickle. Top with the avocado slices and cheese, then the ham. Sandwich together with the remaining slices and press down firmly.

Break the eggs into a shallow wide dish and beat with a fork to combine. Carefully place the sandwiches in the beaten egg and turn to coat both sides. The bread will absorb the egg.

Heat a little oil and butter in a large non-stick frying pan over a high heat. Add the sandwiches and fry for 3–4 minutes on each side, until lightly golden and the filling has just melted.

Slice each one in half and serve hot.

TOASTED BRIOCHE WITH AVOCADO, SPINACH AND BACON

*Leave out the bacon for veggies. Full of flavour, the sweetness
of the brioche makes this a delicious brunch dish. For those
who love chilli, add a splash of chilli sauce to serve.*

MAKES 8 HALVES

8 rashers of back bacon

8 clusters of cherry
    tomatoes on the vine

3 tbsp full-fat
    cream cheese

½ × jar mango chutney
    (approx. 150g/5oz)

A little sunflower oil

150g (5oz) baby spinach

1 garlic clove, crushed

4 brioche buns,
    sliced in half

2 avocados, peeled
    and thinly sliced

Mary's Tips

* Best served and made.
* Not suitable for freezing.

Preheat the oven to 200°C/180°C Fan/Gas 6. Line
a baking sheet with non-stick baking paper.

Arrange the bacon on the baking sheet. Cook in
the oven for about 5–7 minutes, until light golden.

Add the cherry tomatoes and continue to cook
for further 8–10 minutes, until the tomatoes have
softened and the bacon is crisp.

Measure the cream cheese and chutney into a small
bowl. Season with salt and freshly ground black
pepper and mix well.

Heat the oil in a non-stick frying pan over a medium
heat. Add the spinach and garlic and fry for few
minutes until just wilted.

Meanwhile, toast the buns and place on a board.
Spread each one with the cream cheese and chutney
mixture, then top with the wilted spinach. Place the
avocado slices on top, and finish with the bacon and
a cluster of tomatoes.

Serve at once.

MATCH DAY HOT DOGS

Great for hungry teenagers and for taking to a sports match. Keep the relish
in a jar, the sausages hot, wrapped tight, and the buns in a basket.

SERVES 6

6 good-quality
    pork sausages
6 hot dog buns

SPICED TOMATO
RELISH

1 tbsp olive oil
2 banana shallots,
    thinly sliced
½ red pepper, deseeded
    and very finely diced
2 tomatoes, finely chopped
2 tsp chipotle paste
2 tsp balsamic glaze
1 tsp brown sugar

Mary's Tips

* *The relish can be made*
  up to a day ahead.
* *Not suitable for freezing.*

Cook the sausages under the grill or however you prefer to cook your sausages until they are golden and cooked through.

Meanwhile, to make the relish, heat the oil in a large saucepan over a high heat. Add the shallots and pepper and fry for 5 minutes, until softened.

Add the tomatoes and cook for about 5 minutes, stirring until they have softened.

Stir in the chipotle paste, balsamic glaze and sugar and mix together. Season with salt and freshly ground black pepper and remove from the heat.

Slice the buns lengthways, place the sausages in the buns and top with the relish.

CHICKEN, AVOCADO AND MANGO LETTUCE WRAPS

These are great to make a pile of and serve on a platter. Use iceberg or romaine lettuce for the outer wrap; both are a firm lettuce so work well and hold their shape. If the core of the lettuce is very thick, cut it out using a small knife.

MAKES 8

6 tbsp mayonnaise

4 heaped tbsp full-fat crème fraîche

2 tsp garam masala

2 tsp ground turmeric

1 tbsp mango chutney

A squeeze of fresh lemon juice

½ ripe mango, peeled and diced

2 cooked skinless and boneless chicken breasts, pulled into thin strips

1 large iceberg lettuce

1 avocado, peeled and sliced

Mary's Tips

* The chicken mixture can be made up to 4 hours ahead – keep refrigerated. Assemble up to 1 hour ahead.

* Not suitable for freezing.

Measure the mayonnaise, crème fraîche, spices, chutney and lemon juice into a bowl. Mix well and season with salt and freshly ground black pepper.

Add the diced mango and chicken strips and toss to coat.

Trim the root end from the iceberg lettuce and carefully peel away the large leaves, keeping them whole, in one piece. You will need 8 large whole leaves.

Place one leaf on a board. Put some of the chicken mixture in the centre of the leaf. Sit a few slices of avocado on top. Fold in the leafy sides and carefully roll up tightly from the core end to make a fat cigar shape. Repeat with the remaining ingredients.

Serve whole or sliced in half.

FRUIT KEBABS WITH LEMON DIP

These are so refreshing for brunch. Choose fruit that is perfectly ripe and naturally sweet. You can tell when a pineapple is ripe because it should smell sweet, and if you pull one of the leaves from the top it will come out easily.

MAKES 6

1 small, ripe pineapple

300g (10½oz) strawberries, hulled and halved if large

300g (10½oz) mango, peeled and cut into 2.5cm (1in) cubes

LEMON DIP

200g (7oz) Greek yoghurt

2 tbsp lemon curd

2 tbsp mint leaves, chopped

A few sprigs of mint, leaves picked, to garnish

Mary's Tips

* *The kebabs can be assembled up to 3 hours ahead. The dip can be made up to a day ahead.*

* *Not suitable for freezing.*

You will need 6 skewers.

Place the pineapple on a board. Remove the top and base and trim away the woody skin. Slice into quarters lengthways and remove the core. Cut the flesh into 2.5cm (1in) cubes.

Thread one pineapple cube on to a skewer. Add one strawberry and a piece of mango. Repeat until there are two of each fruit on every skewer.

Meanwhile, mix the yoghurt, lemon curd and chopped mint together in a small bowl.

Arrange the kebabs on a long platter with the dip alongside.

Garnish with mint leaves to serve.

SHARING

CORIANDER ROASTED VEGETABLES WITH BASIL OLIVE DIP

Perfect for a leisurely weekend lunch. Serve this with your favourite bread, such as pitta, focaccia or ciabatta. These go well with the Halloumi and Sweet Potato Fries on page 86 and the Bresaola Sharing Board on page 64.

SERVES 6

1 small cauliflower, broken into florets

3 tbsp olive oil

1 tbsp ground coriander

2 red peppers, deseeded and each cut into 6 large wedges

175g (6oz) baby corn, halved lengthways

4 celery sticks, cut into batons

BASIL OLIVE DIP

Small bunch of basil, leaves picked

Small bunch of coriander, leaves picked

70g (2½oz) pitted black olives, halved

2 garlic cloves, quartered

55g (2oz) Parmesan, coarsely grated

Juice of 1 large lemon

75ml (2½fl oz) olive oil

Mary's Tips

* *Can be assembled up to 6 hours ahead. Dip can be made up to a day ahead.*

* *Not suitable for freezing.*

You will need a long wooden board or large platter.

Preheat the oven 220°C/200°C Fan/Gas 7.

Place the cauliflower in a large bowl, toss in 1 tablespoon of the olive oil and sprinkle with the ground coriander. Season with salt and freshly ground black pepper, then tip into one end of a large roasting tin in a single layer.

Place the pepper pieces and baby corn into separate bowls, season and toss with the remaining oil. Tip the pepper into the tin alongside the cauliflower and roast them both in the oven for 5–10 minutes. Remove the tin from the oven and add the baby corn. Return the tin to the oven to roast for a final 10 minutes, until the vegetables are tender and brown but not too soft.

Meanwhile, to make the basil olive dip, place the herbs, olives, garlic, Parmesan and lemon juice in a food processor and whiz for few seconds. Gradually pour in the oil, whizzing all the time, until combined. Season and whiz again to a coarse dipping mixture.

Arrange the vegetables on a sharing board and place the celery sticks and dip alongside.

Serve with slices of bread or Garlic Parsley Flatbread (see page 85).

BRESAOLA SHARING BOARD WITH ROCKET, PARMESAN AND BEAN SALAD

Bresaola is cured beef. Deep and dark in colour with a strong flavour, it is delicious with peppery rocket leaves. You could use prosciutto crudo instead, if preferred, which is dry cured pork.

SERVES 6

30 slices bresaola
115g (4oz) rocket leaves
55g (2oz) Parmesan, shaved

BEAN SALAD

2 × 400g tins cannellini beans, rinsed and drained well
½ red onion, very finely chopped
Small bunch of flat-leaf parsley, chopped
70g (2½oz) green pitted olives, finely sliced
2 garlic cloves, crushed
Zest of ½ lemon and juice of 1 lemon
6 tbsp olive oil
A good pinch of caster sugar

DRESSING

2 tbsp olive oil
2 tbsp balsamic glaze

Mary's Tips

* Can be assembled up to 6 hours ahead. Cover to prevent drying out.
* Bean salad can be made up to 8 hours ahead.
* Not suitable for freezing.

You will need a long wooden board or large platter.

To make the bean salad, tip the cannellini beans into a bowl and add all the remaining ingredients. Toss everything together and season well with salt and freshly ground black pepper.

Arrange the bresaola slices on a sharing board or large platter. Pile up the rocket and scatter with shavings of Parmesan. Place the bean salad on the other side of the rocket.

Season everything with sea salt and freshly ground black pepper and drizzle with the olive oil and balsamic glaze to serve.

SMOKED SALMON AND BURRATA SHARING PLATTER

*A wonderful sharing board of fresh vibrant flavours. Smoked salmon,
smoked trout or gravadlax can be used. When buying the tomatoes,
choose different colours and sizes. When served on a board or platter,
this looks so attractive and is perfect for passing round the table.*

SERVES 6

225g (8oz) asparagus
  spears
500g (1lb 2oz) heritage
  tomatoes, different
  colours and sizes,
  sliced or quartered
  depending on size
½ bunch of basil,
  roughly chopped
1 × 150g (5oz) ball
  burrata, well drained
200g (7oz) slices
  smoked salmon
½ cucumber, peeled, halved
  lengthways, deseeded
  and sliced into crescents
1 lemon, sliced
  into wedges

DRESSING

2 tbsp white wine vinegar
2 tbsp balsamic glaze
1 tbsp runny honey
2 tsp Dijon or
  grainy mustard
125ml (4fl oz) olive oil

Mary's Tips

* *Can be assembled up to
  4 hours ahead. Dress
  just before serving.*
* *Not suitable for freezing.*

You will need a long wooden board or large platter.

Remove the woody ends from the asparagus. Cook
the asparagus in a pan of boiling salted water for
3–4 minutes. Drain and refresh under cold water.
Drain again and set aside.

Arrange the tomatoes at one end of the board and
sprinkle with half the basil. Place the asparagus next
to the tomatoes and the burrata next to the spears.
Curl the slices of smoked salmon alongside.

Mix the cucumber with the remaining basil and
season with salt. Pile the cucumber next to the
smoked salmon at the far end of the board and
sprinkle freshly ground black pepper all over.
Arrange the lemon wedges alongside.

Measure all the dressing ingredients into a jug.
Season and stir until well mixed. Drizzle some
over the platter and serve the rest alongside.

Finally, sprinkle the tomatoes with sea salt and
serve with bread rolls.

HARISSA HALLOUMI AND SQUASH SKEWERS

Cut the halloumi and squash into equal-sized cubes so they cook evenly.

MAKES 6

225g (8oz) butternut
  squash, peeled and
  cut into 18 cubes, each
  2–3cm (¾–1¼in)
1 red pepper, deseeded
  and sliced into 18 pieces
1 × 250g (9oz) halloumi
  block, cut into 12 cubes
2 tbsp sunflower oil
1 tsp harissa paste
1 garlic clove, crushed
2 tbsp runny honey
Juice of ½ lemon

Mary's Tips

* Can be assembled up
  to 8 hours ahead.
* Not suitable for freezing.
* Cook well on the
  barbecue.
* These should be a
  beautiful, rich glazed
  colour. If you brush
  the skewers with the
  harissa glaze at the
  start of cooking, they
  may end up too dark.

You will need 6 wooden skewers, soaked in cold water for 30 minutes. (This prevents them from burning when cooking.)

Preheat the grill to high and line a baking sheet with foil.

Blanch the squash in boiling salted water for 6–7 minutes. Drain and refresh under cold water, then drain again well.

Thread 3 cubes of squash, 3 pieces of pepper and 2 cubes of halloumi on to each wooden skewer in a random order. Place on the baking sheet and brush with oil, so they are well coated.

Mix the harissa paste, garlic, honey and lemon juice together in a small bowl.

Grill the skewers for 2–3 minutes. Turn over and grill for another 2–3 minutes, until the squash is tender and starting to colour.

Brush the skewers with the harissa mixture and return to the grill for a final 1½ minutes, until golden and starting to char.

Serve at once (see photo on pages 70–1).

BLACK BEAN
CHICKEN SKEWERS

*Marinated chicken kebabs, bursting with Asian flavours. Black
bean sauce is readily available to buy in bottles.*

MAKES 12

3 tbsp black bean sauce

1 tsp finely grated
fresh root ginger

1 tsp sesame oil

2 tsp runny honey

2 small skinless and
boneless chicken
breasts, each sliced
into 6 long strips

Mary's Tips

* Can be marinated up
to 8 hours ahead.

* Freeze well marinated.

* Cook well on the
barbecue.

* You could make small
versions these as canapés,
by cutting the skewers
and chicken strips in half
to make them shorter.

You will need 6 wooden skewers, soaked in cold water
for 30 minutes. (This prevents them from burning
when cooking.)

Measure the black bean sauce, grated ginger, sesame
oil and honey into a bowl. Season with salt and freshly
ground black pepper and stir to mix.

Add the chicken strips and stir to coat. Marinate for
about 30 minutes.

Preheat the grill to high and line a baking sheet
with foil.

Thread the chicken strips on to the skewers and
arrange in a single layer on the baking sheet. Grill
the chicken on the highest grill shelf for 5–6 minutes,
until golden on both sides and cooked through.

Serve at once (see photo on pages 70–1).

HONEY-GLAZED SALMON AND COURGETTE SKEWERS

Kebab skewers are great for sharing and a good way to serve different flavours. Cut the cubes all the same size so they cook at the same rate. These are good on the barbecue.

MAKES 6

300g (10½oz) salmon fillet, skinned and cut into 12 even-sized cubes

1 courgette, trimmed, halved lengthways and sliced into 18 pieces

6 cherry tomatoes

2 tbsp sunflower oil

MARINADE

3 tbsp soy sauce

1 tbsp runny honey

1 garlic clove, crushed

2 tsp light muscovado sugar

Juice of ½ lemon

Splash of white wine vinegar

Mary's Tips

* *Can be assembled up to 8 hours ahead.*

* *Not suitable for freezing.*

* *Cook well on the barbecue.*

You will need 6 wooden skewers, soaked in cold water for 30 minutes. (This prevents them from burning when cooking.)

To make the marinade, measure the soy, honey, garlic, sugar, lemon juice and vinegar into a wide bowl. Stir well to mix.

Place the salmon and courgette in the bowl. Stir to coat, then leave to marinate for 30 minutes.

Preheat the grill to high and line a baking sheet with foil.

Thread 2 cubes of salmon, 3 pieces of courgette and 1 tomato on to each skewer, alternating the ingredients. Place them on the baking sheet and grill on the top shelf for 4–5 minutes on each side, until the salmon and courgettes are coloured and cooked through.

Meanwhile, pour any leftover marinade into a small saucepan and bring up to the boil. Reduce by half to a sticky glaze.

Arrange the skewers on a plate and pour the sauce over to serve (see photo on pages 70–1).

MINTED LAMB KOFTA WITH CUCUMBER DIP

With mint and a hint of cumin, these koftas are quick to make and great to share. A kofta can be made using any minced meat, but usually lamb, and the addition of spice makes them of Asian heritage. They are traditionally oval, but you could do round balls. Serve them with the Greek Salad on page 194.

SERVES 4

Vegetable oil, for frying

LAMB KOFTA

1 red onion, chopped

55g (2oz) breadcrumbs

400g (14oz) lean minced lamb

2 tsp mint sauce

½ large bunch of mint, chopped

2 tsp ground cumin

1 garlic clove, crushed

CUCUMBER DIP

200g (7oz) Greek yoghurt

½ large bunch of mint, chopped

55g (2oz) cucumber, deseeded and very finely sliced

Mary's Tips

* *Koftas can be made up to a day ahead.*
* *Raw koftas freeze well.*

To make the koftas, measure all the ingredients into a food processor. Season with salt and freshly ground black pepper and whiz until the mixture has come together. Remove the mixture and, using wet hands, shape into 16 small oval koftas.

Heat a little oil in a large frying pan. Add the koftas and fry over a medium-high heat for about 10 minutes, until golden brown all over and cooked through. Drain on kitchen paper.

Meanwhile, to make the dip, measure the ingredients into a bowl. Season and stir to combine.

Serve the koftas with the cucumber dip alongside.

BEEF KOFTA WITH TOMATO SALSA

These kofta are full of flavour and spice and are good served with salad or pitta breads. Omit the pistachios for friends with a nut allergy.

SERVES 4

Vegetable oil, for frying

BEEF KOFTA

55g (2oz) breadcrumbs
400g (14oz) lean
    minced beef
1 heaped tsp finely grated
    fresh root ginger
2 garlic cloves, crushed
2 tsp harissa paste
2 tsp ground cinnamon
1½ tbsp ground cumin
Juice of ½ lime
Small bunch of flat-leaf
    parsley, chopped
30g (1oz) pistachios, shelled
    and roughly chopped

TOMATO SALSA

250g (9oz) cherry tomatoes
2 tbsp chopped red onion
1 large garlic clove, crushed
1½ tbsp sun-dried
    tomato paste
2 tsp harissa paste
A good pinch of sugar
Juice of ½ lime

Mary's Tips

* *Koftas can be made up to
    a day ahead. Dip can be
    made up to 2 days ahead.*
* *Raw koftas freeze well.*

To make the koftas, measure all the ingredients into a food processor. Season with salt and freshly ground black pepper and whiz until combined. Add the breadcrumbs and whiz again. Remove the mixture from the processor and, using wet hands, shape into 16 oval koftas.

Heat a little oil in a large frying pan. Add the koftas and fry for 8–10 minutes, turning until cooked through and golden all over.

Meanwhile, place the salsa ingredients in a clean food processor and pulse until finely chopped. Season, then spoon into a small bowl.

Serve the koftas with the tomato salsa alongside.

SPICED BEEF WITH CHICORY

This is great as a sharing plate and very easy to make ahead. Luce used to make a similar dish years ago and we thought it deserved a comeback. Use Little Gem leaves if you can't get red chicory.

SERVES 6

2 tbsp olive or sesame oil

450g (1lb) lean
    minced beef

2cm (¾in) piece of
    fresh root ginger,
    peeled and grated

2 garlic cloves, crushed

2 shallots, finely chopped

1 tbsp Chinese five
    spice powder

A pinch of dried
    chilli flakes

3 tbsp soy sauce

2 tbsp hoisin sauce

4 tbsp chopped
    fresh coriander

24 red chicory
    leaves, trimmed

Soured cream, to serve

Small bunch of coriander,
    leaves picked, to serve

Mary's Tips

* *The mince can be made
    up to a day ahead.*

* *Freezes well.*

* *If you are a chilli
    fan, sprinkle red chilli
    on the soured cream
    before serving.*

Heat the oil in large non-stick frying pan over a high heat. Add the minced beef and fry for 4–5 minutes, breaking the mince with two wooden spoons as it is frying, until golden brown.

Add the ginger, garlic, shallots, five spice powder, chilli flakes and soy and fry for a minute. Season with freshly ground black pepper, cover and cook over a gentle heat for about 25–30 minutes, until cooked.

Stir in the hoisin sauce and check the seasoning. Add the coriander and set aside.

Arrange the leaves on a large platter and spoon the mince into the centre of each leaf.

Top with a little blob of soured cream and a coriander leaf, and serve immediately.

TUNA CEVICHE WITH PICKLED GINGER AND SALSA

*Ceviche is marinated fish or seafood. Only use the freshest sustainable fish.
The marinating liquid is usually lime or lemon, which causes
the raw fish to turn opaque. If you enjoy sushi, give this a try.
Wasabi is a very hot Japanese horseradish-style paste.*

SERVES 6

500g (1lb 2oz) raw
  tuna, skinned and
  cut into strips about
  1 × 8cm (½ × 3¼in)
Juice of 2 large limes
2 tbsp soy sauce
3 tbsp pickled ginger
2 tbsp coriander leaves
55g (2oz) pea shoots
2 tbsp sesame seeds

SALSA

1 green chilli, deseeded
  and finely chopped
½ small red onion,
  finely chopped
3 large tomatoes, deseeded
  and finely diced
50ml (2fl oz) olive oil
2 tbsp chopped coriander

Mary's Tips

* *The platter can be
  arranged up to 4
  hours ahead and
  kept in the fridge.*
* *Not suitable for freezing.*

Place the tuna strips into a bowl and pour over
the lime juice and soy. Turn so all the fish is coated.
Transfer to the fridge for about an hour.

Meanwhile, to make the salsa, place the chilli,
onion and tomatoes into a bowl and season with
salt and freshly ground black pepper. Add the oil
and coriander and mix well.

Drain the fish from the soy and lime juice and add
the soy and lime mixture to the salsa. Toss everything
together and spoon into a small serving bowl.

Place the pickled ginger in another small serving bowl.

Arrange the coriander leaves and pea shoots in a
pile in the centre of each plate. Lay the strips of
tuna beside the leaves and sprinkle the tuna with the
sesame seeds.

Serve the tuna at room temperature with the salsa and
pickled ginger alongside.

SECRETS OF SUSHI

The secret of good sushi is to make good sticky rice. I have given you a simple method for making it and, nowadays, the sushi rice you buy from supermarkets has good instructions on the side of the packet. A 500g (1lb 2oz) packet of rice will be enough for both the following recipes. It takes a little while to prepare, so it would be very annoying to run out – therefore I use the whole packet!

To make the sushi you will need a bowl of vinegar water (water with a little vinegar in it) – this is important as the rice is so sticky, you'll need to dip your hands in the water before handling the rice. To make the rolls you will also need a bamboo rolling mat – they are readily available and worth buying if you enjoy this recipe. Nori are flat sheets of dried seaweed.

SIMPLE SUSHI RICE

500g (1lb 2oz) uncooked
   sushi rice
60ml (4 tbsp) rice
   wine vinegar
50ml (2fl oz) mirin or sake
½ tsp salt

Mary's Tip

* *To cool the sushi rice
quickly, spread out on a
large tray or baking sheet.*

Place the rice in a bowl. Cover with cold water and stir to release the starch. Rinse and drain 4–5 times, until the water is clear. Cover with cold water and leave to soak for 20 minutes.

Drain the rice and place in a saucepan. Add 700ml (1¼ pints) cold water, cover and place over a high heat. Bring up to the boil, reduce the heat and simmer over a very low heat for 10 minutes. Remove from the heat and leave for another 10 minutes.

Meanwhile, mix the vinegar, mirin or sake and salt in a small bowl. Use a knife or firm spatula to fold the vinegar mixture gently into the rice. Continue to cut and fold through the rice while cooling with a fan or firm piece of card (it is important to cool the rice quickly, so it stays sticky).

Once it is cold, it is ready to use. Use all the rice on the same day it is made.

HOSO MAKI

Thin rolled sushi are one of the most popular sushi dishes. Swap the crabmeat with spring onions, carrot sticks, cucumber sticks, or celery sticks halved lengthways for vegetarians. Wasabi is very hot so use as little or as much as you like.

MAKES 24

3 sheets nori (seaweed)

Vinegar water (see opposite)

About 500g (1lb 2oz) cooked sushi rice (see opposite)

1 tbsp wasabi, plus extra to serve

115g (4oz) fresh white crabmeat

½ short cucumber, halved lengthways, deseeded and cut into long thin strips

Soy sauce, to serve

Mary's Tip

* *The rolls can be made ahead and wrapped in cling film before slicing.*

You will need a bamboo rolling mat.

Place the rolling mat on a flat surface and lay a sheet of nori shiny side down on top of the mat. Dip your hands in the vinegar water, then take about 175g (6oz) sushi rice and spread over the nori to cover, leaving a 2.5cm (1in) gap along the edge furthest away from you.

Make a shallow trench with the side of your hand along the centre of the rice (from left to right). Spread a thin layer of wasabi about 1cm (½in) wide along the trench. Cover the wasabi with a third crabmeat and place a line of cucumber strips either side of the crab. Moisten the unfilled edge of nori with a little cold water and, using the rolling mat, roll from the edge nearest to you, squeezing to make a tight roll. Seal the moistened edge around the roll.

Dampen a very sharp knife, trim off the ends and slice each roll into 8 pieces. A gentle sawing action works well here, to keep the sushi roll in a perfect shape. Continue with the remaining nori and filling.

Serve with a small bowl of soy sauce and some wasabi alongside (see photo on page 80).

SUSHI SQUARES WITH SMOKED SALMON AND PICKLED GINGER

The easiest way to make these squares is by pushing the rice into a small 18 × 18cm (7 × 7in) toffee tin. If you do not have one, shape them on a board.

MAKES 36

Vinegar water (see page 78)

About 500g (1lb 2oz) cooked sushi rice (see page 78)

4 slices smoked salmon

A few strips of pickled ginger from a jar, roughly chopped

Mary's Tip

* Lightly wet the inside of the tin before lining – this helps the cling film stay in place.

Line a small 18 × 18cm (7 × 7in) toffee tin with cling film.

Dip your hands in vinegar water and place handfuls of rice into the tin, pressing firmly, and level the surface. Place in the fridge for about 30 minutes, or until chilled and very firm.

Turn the tin upside down on to a board and remove the cling film. Use a large, sharp knife to cut it into 36 small, neat squares and transfer to a serving plate.

Cut the smoked salmon into matching squares and place them on top of the rice.

Garnish with a little pickled ginger to serve.

GARLIC PARSLEY FLATBREAD

This quick and easy flatbread has a crisp base. Vary your topping as you wish –
add feta or goat's cheese, sun-dried tomatoes or olives. Make double the quantity
of garlic butter and shape half into a roll, wrap in non-stick baking paper and
freeze. Slice straight from the freezer and serve melted over meat or fish.

CUTS INTO
8 WEDGES

FLATBREAD

175g (6oz) self-raising
    flour, plus extra
    for dusting
½ tsp fine sea salt
1 medium egg
70ml (2½fl oz) milk

TOPPING

75g (3oz) butter, softened
4 large garlic cloves,
    crushed
2 tbsp chopped
    flat-leaf parsley
30g (1oz) mature Cheddar
    or Parmesan, grated

Mary's Tips

* *Can be assembled up*
  to 2 hours ahead.

* *Not suitable for freezing.*

* *Make sure the butter*
  is very soft so that it
  doesn't pull the dough
  as it is spread over.

Preheat the oven to 220°C/200°C Fan/Gas 7. Slide
a large baking sheet into the oven to get hot.

Measure the flour into a large bowl and add the salt.
Beat the egg and milk together in a small jug, then
pour into the flour and mix to form a soft dough.

Tip the dough out on to a floured work surface and
knead gently. Shape into a smooth ball and place it
on a large piece of non-stick baking paper. Roll
out the dough using a rolling pin to a large round
measuring about 30cm (12in) diameter.

Mix the butter, garlic, parsley and a little sea salt
together in a bowl. Spread the garlic butter carefully
over the dough base, then sprinkle with the cheese.

Holding the baking paper, carefully transfer to the hot
baking sheet and bake in the preheated oven for about
12 minutes, until golden and crisp underneath.

Slice into wedges and serve at once.

HALLOUMI AND SWEET POTATO FRIES WITH CHILLI DIP

These are so popular with the young, and are great for sharing. Serve the fries in little bowls or buckets, like you get in trendy bars! The fries go well with the Bresaola Sharing Board (see page 64) and the Coriander Roasted Vegetables sharing board (see page 63).

SERVES 6

SWEET POTATO FRIES

3 large sweet potatoes (each about 250g/9oz), peeled and cut into long thin chips, about 8cm (3¼in) long and 1cm (½in) thick

2 tbsp olive oil

2 tbsp cornflour

2 tsp sweet smoked paprika

HALLOUMI FRIES

2 × 250g (9oz) blocks halloumi, drained

2–3 tbsp olive oil

40g (1½oz) panko breadcrumbs

CHILLI DIP

2 tbsp full-fat crème fraîche

2 tbsp mayonnaise

2 tbsp sweet chilli sauce

1 red chilli, deseeded and finely chopped

A good squeeze of fresh lemon juice

2 tbsp chopped chives

Mary's Tips

* *Dip can be made up to a day ahead.*

Preheat the oven 220°C/200°C Fan/Gas 7. You will need a large baking sheet and a large roasting tin.

Tip the sweet potato chips into a large bowl, add the olive oil, cornflour and paprika and toss to coat. Scatter into the roasting tin and spread out evenly.

Cut each block of halloumi in half horizontally and slice each half lengthways into 4 rectangular sticks. You should have 16 chips in total. Brush them with olive oil, then toss in the breadcrumbs to coat. Place the sticks on the baking sheet in a single layer.

Slide the sweet potato fries on to the top shelf of the oven and cook for about 15 minutes. Turn over, and return to the oven with the halloumi. Cook both together for a further 15–20 minutes, until crisp and golden.

Meanwhile, to make the chilli dip, mix all the ingredients together and season with salt and freshly ground black pepper.

Tip the fries into individual containers and serve with the chilli dip alongside.

JUMBO SAUSAGE ROLLS

These jumbo rolls look great and, with thyme and mustard, have great flavour, too. Choose sausages that are family favourites; I like gourmet pork and leek.

MAKES 2

4 good-quality pork sausages

½ dessert apple, peeled, cored and coarsely grated

2 tsp chopped thyme leaves

1 tbsp grainy mustard

2 tbsp chopped flat-leaf parsley

1 × 375g packet of ready-rolled all-butter puff pastry

1 egg, beaten

Mary's Tips

* Can be made up to a day ahead and reheated in a hot oven to serve.

* Freeze well cooked.

Preheat the oven to 220°C/200°C Fan/Gas 7 and line a large baking sheet with non-stick baking paper.

Remove the sausage meat from the skins. Place the sausage meat in a mixing bowl and add the apple, thyme, mustard and parsley. Season well with salt and freshly ground black pepper and mash together with a fork until combined.

Unroll the pastry with a long edge nearest to you. Cut the pastry in half horizontally to make two rectangles. Brush the pastry, all over, with the beaten egg.

Spoon half of the sausage mixture along a long edge about 4cm (1½in) in from the edge in a sausage shape. Fold the pastry over the sausage mixture and press down to encase it (making a long sausage roll). Press down on the seal with a fork to make a neat edge. Repeat with the remaining pastry and sausage mixture to make a second roll.

Place the rolls on the baking sheet and glaze with the remaining egg. Bake in the preheated oven for about 25 minutes, until golden and crisp.

Serve warm with mustard mayonnaise or ketchup.

JUMBO LENTIL ROLLS

These are like the Jumbo Sausage Rolls (see page 88) but with a veggie filling of lentils, goat's cheese and herbs. They became huge favourites when we were testing the recipes for the book. It was a total surprise that they were such a big hit! Perfect for sharing – wrap them up and give to friends. These would be great enjoyed at an outside event, but they must be served warm.

MAKES 2

125g (4½oz) dried
   Puy lentils
115g (4oz) soft
   goat's cheese
115g (4oz) sun-blushed
   tomatoes, chopped
3 tbsp chopped mint
55g (2oz) mature Cheddar,
   coarsely grated
2 tsp ground cumin
1 × 375g packet of
   ready-rolled all-
   butter puff pastry
1 egg, beaten

Mary's Tips

* *Can be made up to a
   day ahead and reheated
   in a hot oven to serve.*

* *Freeze well cooked.*

Preheat the oven to 220°C/200°C Fan/Gas 7 and line a large baking sheet with non-stick baking paper.

Place the lentils in a saucepan, cover with cold water and bring up to boil. Reduce the heat and simmer gently for about 20 minutes until tender (or cook according to the packet instructions). Drain and leave to cool.

Place the cooked lentils in a mixing bowl. Add the goat's cheese, sun-blushed tomatoes, mint, Cheddar and ground cumin, season well with salt and freshly ground black pepper and stir to combine.

Unroll the pastry, with a long edge nearest to you. Cut the pastry in half horizontally to make two rectangles. Brush the pastry, all over, with the beaten egg.

Spoon half of the lentil mixture along a long edge about 4cm (1½in) in from the edge. Fold the pastry over the lentil mixture and press down to encase it (making a long lentil roll). Press down on the seal with a fork to make a neat edge. Repeat with the remaining pastry and lentil mixture to make a second roll.

Place the rolls on the baking sheet and glaze with the remaining beaten egg. Bake in the preheated oven for about 25 minutes, until golden and crisp.

Serve warm with salad.

FISH

SMOKED HADDOCK MACARONI CHEESE

*Pairing the nation's favourite mac'n'cheese with smoked haddock
is a winning combination. Panko breadcrumbs are light and
crisp Japanese breadcrumbs that add lots of crunch.*

SERVES 6

200g (7oz) macaroni
40g (1½oz) butter
40g (1½oz) plain flour
900ml (1½ pints) hot milk
250g (9oz) mature
    Cheddar, grated
2 tsp Dijon mustard
500g (1lb 2oz) undyed
    smoked haddock fillet,
    skinned and cut into
    3cm (1¼in) cubes
125g (4½oz) frozen
    petits pois
40g (1½oz) panko
    breadcrumbs

Mary's Tips

* *Can be made up to
  8 hours ahead.*

* *Freezes well with an
  extra 100ml (3½fl
  oz) hot milk added
  to the sauce.*

Preheat the oven to 200°C/180°C Fan/Gas 6. You
will need a deep 2.2 litre (3¾ pint) ovenproof dish.

Cook the pasta in boiling salted water according to
the packet instructions. Drain and refresh under
cold water. Drain again and set aside.

Melt the butter in a saucepan over a medium heat.
Add the flour and stir for a few seconds. Gradually
whisk in the hot milk and continue to whisk until
smooth and thickened.

Remove from the heat and stir in half the Cheddar
and the Dijon mustard. Season well with salt and
freshly ground black pepper.

Add the cooked macaroni, haddock and frozen peas.
Stir well and spoon into the ovenproof dish. Mix the
panko breadcrumbs with the remaining cheese and
sprinkle over the top in an even layer. Bake in the
preheated oven for 25–30 minutes, until golden on
top and the fish is cooked through.

Serve hot with some green veg.

MISO SALMON
WITH AROMATIC SPINACH

A simple salmon fillet with miso marinade – quick to do and super healthy.

SERVES 4

4 × 150g (5oz) salmon
fillets, skinned (use
even-sized middle fillets
so they all cook evenly)

1 tbsp sunflower oil

A knob of butter

2 large banana shallots,
finely chopped

1 heaped tsp finely grated
fresh root ginger

470g (1lb 1oz)
baby spinach

MISO MARINADE

3 tbsp white miso paste

1½ tbsp sesame oil

1½ tbsp soy sauce

Juice of ½ lemon

3 tbsp runny honey

1 large garlic clove,
crushed

1 heaped tsp finely grated
fresh root ginger

Mary's Tips

* Marinade can be made
up to 4 hours ahead.

* Not suitable for freezing.

Measure all the miso marinade ingredients into a small bowl. Whisk everything together to make a smooth consistency. Pour half of the marinade into a shallow dish and reserve the rest.

Place the fillets into the dish with the marinade, turn to coat, then cover with cling film and leave to marinate for 30–60 minutes in the fridge.

Preheat the oven to 200°C/180°C Fan/Gas 6 and line a baking sheet with non-stick baking paper.

Heat a frying pan over a high heat until very hot. Drizzle the sunflower oil over the salmon fillets and season with freshly ground black pepper. Place the fillets in the pan and fry on the top side only for 20–30 seconds, until browned but still raw.

Place the fillets browned side up on the prepared baking sheet and transfer to the oven for 12–15 minutes, until the salmon is opaque in the centre.

Pour the reserved marinade into a saucepan. Add 150ml (¼ pint) water and bring up to the boil. Reduce slightly, then turn down the heat and keep warm.

Meanwhile, cook the spinach. Heat the butter in a large frying pan over a medium heat. Add the shallots and fry for 3–4 minutes, until softened. Add the ginger and fry for 1 minute. Add the spinach and fry quickly until just wilted. Season well.

Arrange the spinach on a serving platter and top with the salmon fillets. Drizzle with a little hot marinade to serve.

SALMON EN CROÛTE
WITH SPINACH AND DILL

*Salmon en croûte is still so popular on the buffet table or when serving
numbers. If you can't find a single piece of salmon that is big enough,
it is possible to use 2 × 500g (1lb 2oz) fillets side by side.*

SERVES 8–10

SPINACH FILLING

225g (8oz) baby spinach
180g (6½oz) full-fat
  cream cheese
1 egg yolk

SALMON

Flour, for dusting
1 × 500g block of
  all-butter puff pastry
1 × 1kg (2¼lb) salmon
  fillet, cut from the centre
  of the fillet, skinned
  and bones removed
Large bunch of
  dill, chopped
1 × 280g jar chargrilled
  mixed peppers in
  oil, drained
1 egg
1 tbsp milk

HERB SAUCE

3 spring onions,
  finely chopped
2 tsp caster sugar
1 tbsp chopped chives
2 tbsp chopped
  flat-leaf parsley
1 tbsp chopped dill
200g (7oz) full-fat
  crème fraîche
Juice of ½ lemon

To make the spinach filling, tip the baby spinach into
a heatproof bowl. Pour boiling water from the kettle
over the spinach to wilt, then drain well. Squeeze
excess water out of the spinach and set aside to cool.

Add the cream cheese and egg yolk to the cold
spinach, season with salt and freshly ground black
pepper and mix to combine.

Place a large piece of baking paper on to the work
surface and dust with flour. Roll the pastry so it is
long enough and wide enough to wrap around the
fillet to enclose it completely. Trim off any excess
pastry and set aside. Place the fillet in the centre of
the pastry. Season and cover with the dill. Lay the
drained peppers over the fish, then spread the spinach
filling evenly on top.

Break the egg into a bowl and add the milk. Whisk
with a fork until smooth.

Brush the pastry all around the fillet with the egg
mixture. Fold the pastry ends up and over the ends of
the fillet, and brush the pastry ends with beaten egg.
Bring the sides of the pastry to meet at the centre top
and crimp the top edge to seal. Brush all over with the
egg to glaze.

Use the pastry trimmings to cut out shapes or letters.
Stick these on to the pastry top to decorate, and brush
with the egg glaze. Chill in the fridge for a minimum
of 30 minutes.

* *Can be assembled up
  to 24 hours ahead and
  kept in the fridge.*
* *Not suitable for freezing.*

Preheat the oven to 220°C/200°C Fan/Gas 7 and place a baking sheet large enough to hold the en croûte in the oven to get very hot.

Carefully slide the en croûte and the baking paper on to the preheated baking sheet. Bake in the preheated oven for 30–35 minutes, until the pastry is golden and cooked on top and underneath.

Allow the salmon to rest for about 15 minutes at room temperature while you make the sauce.

Measure all the sauce ingredients into a bowl, season and stir to combine.

Carve the salmon into thick slices and serve with the sauce alongside (see photo on pages 100–101).

HOT-SMOKED SALMON RICE AND ASPARAGUS SALAD

Hot-smoked salmon is like poached salmon but with a smoky flavour – perfect for salads. Alternatively, you could use poached salmon. The lemon dressing and herbs make the salad vibrant and bursting with flavour.

SERVES 6

300g (10½oz) mixed white and wild rice (see intro)

6 spring onions, finely sliced

Large bunch of dill, chopped

Large bunch of flat-leaf parsley, chopped

3 eggs

200g (7oz) asparagus spears

200g (7oz) hot-smoked salmon slices, broken into large chunks

LEMON DRESSING

Zest of 1 lemon

Juice of 2 lemons

180ml (6½fl oz) olive oil

4 tbsp white wine vinegar

4 tbsp runny honey

2 tbsp Dijon mustard

Mary's Tips

* *Can be assembled up to 4 hours ahead (including dressing the rice).*

* *Not suitable for freezing.*

Cook the rice in boiling salted water according to the packet instructions. Drain and refresh under cold water. Drain again.

Place the rice in a bowl. Add the spring onions, dill and parsley and season well with salt and freshly ground black pepper. Stir to combine.

Measure all the dressing ingredients into a jug and whisk together well. Reserve 2 tablespoons of the dressing and pour the remainder over the rice. Mix well, cover with cling film and chill in the fridge for about an hour.

Meanwhile, place the eggs in a pan of boiling water and cook for 8 minutes for soft boiled. Drain and place in cold water before peeling. Cut each egg into quarters.

Remove the woody ends from the asparagus. If the spears are thick, cut them in half lengthways. Slice the spears into 5cm lengths, then cook in boiling water for 3 minutes. Drain and refresh under cold water. Drain again.

Tip the asparagus into the rice and mix to combine. Spoon into a serving dish and arrange the salmon pieces and egg quarters on top. Sprinkle with a little salt and freshly ground black pepper, then drizzle over the reserved dressing to serve.

SMOKED HADDOCK AND CELERIAC AND POTATO MASH FISH PIE

A hearty and perfect family fish pie. Using smoked haddock gives a wonderful smoky flavour to the pie but you could use unsmoked haddock, if you prefer.

SERVES 6

4 eggs

75g (3oz) butter

2 leeks, trimmed and thinly sliced

75g (3oz) plain flour

600ml (1 pint) hot milk

150ml (¼ pint) pouring double cream

1 tbsp grainy mustard

Juice of ½ lemon

55g (2oz) Parmesan, grated

750g (1lb 10oz) smoked haddock fillet, skinned and cut into 4cm (1½in) cubes

250g (9oz) baby spinach

TOPPING

600g (1lb 6oz) potatoes, peeled and cut into 3cm (1¼in) cubes

600g (1lb 6oz) celeriac, peeled and cut into 3cm (1¼in) cubes

A knob of butter

About 2 tbsp milk

115g (4oz) Gruyère cheese, grated

Mary's Tips

* *Can be assembled up to 8 hours ahead.*

* *Freezes well without the hard-boiled eggs.*

Preheat the oven to 200°C/180°C Fan/Gas 6. You will need a 1.8 litre (3 pint) ovenproof dish.

To make the topping, cook the potatoes and celeriac in boiling salted water for about 15 minutes until tender. Drain and season with salt and freshly ground black pepper. Mash with the butter and enough milk to make a spreadable consistency. Set aside.

Place the eggs in a pan and cover with water. Bring up to the boil and boil for 8 minutes. Drain and place in cold water before peeling. Cut each egg into quarters.

Meanwhile, melt the butter in a large saucepan over a medium heat. Add the leeks and gently cook for 5 minutes, until soft. Sprinkle in the flour and stir over the heat for 30 seconds. Blend in the hot milk, whisking until smooth. Add the cream, mustard, lemon and Parmesan and stir until combined. Add the fish and simmer for 2 minutes. Season well and spoon into the overproof dish. Arrange the egg quarters over the surface, pushing them gently into the sauce.

Place the spinach in a pan over a medium heat and cook for couple of minutes until just wilted. Season lightly and squeeze out as much liquid as possible. Arrange in 6 piles on top of the fish pie, then spread over the potato and celeriac mash and fork the top. Sprinkle with the Gruyère and bake for 35–40 minutes, until bubbling around the edges and golden brown.

Leave to stand for 5 minutes before serving hot with green vegetables.

MOULES MARINIÈRE

A classic and the ultimate sharing dish. Two bowls of moules in the centre of a table, with crusty bread or sweet potato fries (see page 86) – perfect. If any mussels are open before cooking, give them a tap. If they close, they are fine; if not, discard them. Likewise discard any that are still closed or broken after cooking. If you can't find 'ready-to-cook' mussels, place the fresh mussels into a large bowl of cold water and scrub to clean them. Remove any beards, which are the stringy threads on the side of the shell. Drain before cooking.

SERVES 2

2 tbsp olive oil

A knob of butter

4 large banana shallots, thinly sliced

4 garlic cloves, crushed

1kg (2¼lb) ready-to-cook fresh mussels

150ml (¼ pint) white wine

150ml (¼ pint) pouring double cream

Juice of ½ lemon

Small bunch of flat-leaf parsley, chopped

Mary's Tips

* *Make and serve immediately.*
* *Not suitable for freezing.*

Heat the oil and butter in a wide-based, deep saucepan over a high heat. Add the shallots and fry for 3–4 minutes to soften. Add the garlic and fry for 10 seconds.

Tip the clean mussels into the pan and stir over the heat. Pour in the wine and bring up to the boil. Cover with a lid and boil for 3–4 minutes, giving the pan a shake every now and again, until the mussels have opened.

Remove the mussels with a slotted spoon and place into a warm dish.

Continue to boil the liquid in the pan over a high heat, until reduced by half (which should take around 5 minutes). Add the cream and boil for a few minutes. Taste and season well with salt and freshly ground black pepper.

Return the mussels to the pan, add the lemon juice and the parsley, and toss everything together.

Serve at once while piping hot.

PRAWN STIR-FRY WITH GINGER, COCONUT AND CHILLI

Full of colour and flavour, this is a quick and easy supper dish. Great for sharing in bowls in the kitchen and it would be good to eat standing up, too!

SERVES 4–6

A large knob of butter

600g (1lb 6oz) large raw prawns, shells removed and de-veined

1 tbsp sunflower oil

2 medium courgettes, peeled into ribbons

1 red chilli, deseeded and finely chopped

115g (4¼oz) baby spinach

Small bunch of coriander, chopped

SAUCE

160ml (5½fl oz) coconut cream

Zest and juice of ½ lime

1 tsp fish sauce

1 tbsp sweet chilli sauce

1 tsp grated fresh root ginger

1 garlic clove, crushed

2 tsp cornflour

Mary's Tips

* *Best made and served.*
* *Not suitable for freezing.*
* *Coconut cream has a higher fat content than milk, which makes a better sauce for this dish.*

First make the sauce. Measure all the ingredients into a jug and whisk together until smooth. Season with a little salt and freshly ground black pepper.

Heat the butter in a large frying pan or wok. Add the prawns and fry over a high heat for 4–5 minutes, until the prawns are pink. Transfer to a plate with any cooking juices.

Return the pan to the heat. Add the oil, courgette ribbons and chilli, and fry for 1 minute. Add the spinach and stir until it has just wilted.

Pour the sauce into the pan and bring to the boil, stirring, until thickened.

Return the prawns to the pan and simmer for 1–2 minutes.

Check the seasoning and sprinkle with the chopped coriander to serve.

SCALLOPS WITH GARLIC KING OYSTER MUSHROOMS AND TARRAGON

King oyster mushrooms are large and bursting with earthy mushroom flavours. They have long stems and when cut through lengthways look very attractive. If you are unable to find them, use the more readily available standard oyster mushrooms.

SERVES 4

2 tbsp sunflower oil

55g (2oz) butter

20 small, trimmed scallops (about 300g/10½oz)

3 large garlic cloves, crushed

350g (12oz) king oyster mushrooms, sliced lengthways

250ml (9fl oz) white wine

300ml (½ pint) pouring double cream

A squeeze of fresh lemon juice

1 tbsp chopped fresh flat-leaf parsley

1 tbsp chopped fresh tarragon

Heat a large frying pan until very hot over a high heat. Add 1 tablespoon of the oil and half the butter. When the butter turns a nutty brown colour, add the scallops, season with salt and freshly ground black pepper and fry for only 20–30 seconds on each side. Be careful not to overcook. Transfer to a plate and keep warm.

Add the remaining oil and butter to the pan. Add the garlic and mushrooms and fry over the high heat for 1–2 minutes. Pour in the wine and boil until the wine has reduced by half. Pour in the cream and reduce until slightly thickened and the mushrooms are just cooked. Add a squeeze of lemon juice, some seasoning and sprinkle in most of the herbs.

Spoon the mushrooms and sauce into 4 shallow bowls. Arrange the scallops on top and garnish with the remaining chopped herbs to serve.

POULTRY

ROASTING TIN SPICED CHICKEN

An all-in-one dish that can be thrown in the oven and cooked all at once.

SERVES 4–6

8 large skinless and
  boneless chicken thighs
  (1kg/2¼lb total weight)
1 fennel bulb, trimmed
  and sliced into 8 wedges
  through the root
2 small red peppers,
  deseeded and sliced
  into large pieces
2 medium sweet potatoes,
  peeled and sliced into
  3cm (1¼in) cubes
2 tbsp olive oil
1 tbsp cornflour

FIVE SPICE MARINADE

4 tbsp mango chutney
2 tsp Chinese five
  spice powder
3 tbsp soy sauce
1 tsp grated fresh
  root ginger
2 garlic cloves, crushed
4 mild peppadew peppers,
  finely chopped
Juice of ½ lemon

Mary's Tips

* *Can be assembled up
  to 4 hours ahead.*
* *Marinated chicken thighs
  can be frozen raw.*
* *Keep fresh root ginger
  in the freezer and grate
  it straight from frozen.*

Measure all the marinade ingredients into a large bowl, season with freshly ground black pepper and mix well. Add the chicken and turn to coat in the mixture. Cover and leave to marinate for 1–2 hours in a cool place or overnight in the fridge.

Preheat the oven to 220°C/200°C Fan/Gas 7.

Blanch the fennel wedges in boiling water for about 5 minutes until softened. Drain well.

Tip the blanched fennel and all the prepared vegetables into a large roasting tin. Drizzle with the oil and season well. Add the chicken and all the marinade and toss everything together to coat the vegetables and meat. Roast in the oven for about 25 minutes.

Remove from the oven and carefully pour the tin juices into a small saucepan. Return the roasting tin to the oven for another 10 minutes, until the chicken and vegetables are tinged brown and cooked through.

Meanwhile, mix the cornflour with 2 tablespoons of water until smooth. Bring the pan juices to the boil and pour in the cornflour mixture. Stir until thickened. If it's a little too thick, add some water until it is coating consistency. Pour the sauce into a jug.

Serve the chicken thighs and vegetables piping hot with the sauce alongside.

ROAST CHICKEN BREAST WITH CREAMY MUSHROOMS AND CABBAGE

A meal in itself, there are no extras needed here. This dish is one you will come back to time and time again. Hispi cabbage is sometimes sold as pointed cabbage.

SERVES 4–6

4 skinless and boneless chicken breasts

2 tsp paprika

4 tbsp olive or sunflower oil

A knob of butter

1 large onion, finely chopped

200g (7oz) button mushrooms, sliced

100ml (3½fl oz) white wine

150ml (¼ pint) pouring double cream

1 small Hispi cabbage, quartered, stalk removed and finely shredded

2 tbsp grainy mustard

Mary's Tips

* *Cook until adding the cabbage up to 6 hours ahead. Add the cabbage when reheating.*

* *Not suitable for freezing.*

Preheat the oven to 200°C/180°C Fan/Gas 6 and line a baking sheet with non-stick baking paper.

Season the chicken breasts with salt and freshly ground black pepper and sprinkle with the paprika.

Place a frying pan over a hight heat until very hot. Add 2 tablespoons of the olive oil and fry the chicken breasts until browned on all sides. Transfer to the baking sheet and roast in the oven for about 20 minutes, until cooked through.

Meanwhile, melt the butter and remaining oil in the frying pan and add the onion. Stir over a high heat, cover and cook over a reduced heat for about 8 minutes, until soft. Add the mushrooms to the pan and fry for 3–4 minutes, until lightly golden.

Pour in the wine and boil for a few minutes to reduce by half. Pour in the cream and reduce by half again.

Stir in the cabbage and simmer in the sauce for 2–3 minutes, until wilted but still with a little crunch. Stir in the mustard and season.

Spoon the vegetables on to a plate. Cut each chicken breast into thick diagonal slices and arrange on top to serve.

TWO ROAST CHICKENS WITH SCALLOPED POTATOES

So often sharing a roast is the best way to spend a Sunday and one chicken is never enough with hungry teenagers around, so try this simple recipe to share with the gang. Chicken is great value but always buy free-range. Get two large birds for those who have big appetites. The scalloped potatoes are cooked in the oven at the same time, which makes it even easier.

SERVES 8

2 oven-ready whole chickens (about 1.75kg/3lb 14oz each)

8 fresh bay leaves

Small bunch of sage leaves

1 large lemon, halved

55g (2oz) butter, softened

1 tbsp paprika

1 large bulb garlic, halved horizontally

150ml (¼ pint) white wine

300ml (½ pint) chicken stock

55g (2oz) plain flour

A little gravy browning (optional)

SCALLOPED POTATOES

1.2kg (2lb 12oz) peeled potatoes, very thinly sliced into discs

1 onion, thinly sliced

55g (2oz) butter, cut into cubes, plus extra for greasing

600ml (1 pint) chicken stock

Preheat the oven to 200°C/180°C Fan/Gas 6 and grease a shallow 1.8 litre (3¼ pint) ovenproof dish.

Place the chickens on a board. Place half the bay leaves, a third of the sage and a lemon half in the cavity of each bird.

Mix the butter and paprika together in a small bowl. Spread over the breasts of the birds and season well with salt and freshly ground black pepper.

Place the remaining sage, garlic, wine and stock into the base of a large roasting tin. Put a large grill rack on top and sit the chickens side by side on the rack.

To make the potato gratin, arrange a layer of sliced potato in the base of the prepared dish. Scatter the onion and a few cubes of butter over the top and pour in a little stock. Season well and repeat the layers, including the stock, finishing with a layer of potato. Cover the dish with buttered foil.

Slide the chickens on to the top shelf of the oven and the potatoes on the shelf below. Roast both for about 1½ hours, removing the foil from the potatoes after 45 minutes. Keep an eye on the chickens – if they are getting too brown, then cover with foil. Once the chickens are golden and cooked through, and the potatoes are tender, remove from the oven.

Cover the chickens and potatoes with foil and set aside while you make the gravy.

Strain the juices and stock from the roasting tin into a jug. Skim off as much fat as possible from the jug and reserve. You will need 450ml (¾ pint) liquid from the roasting tin; add extra stock if you need to increase the amount.

Return the fat to the roasting tin and sprinkle in the flour. Stir over the heat for a few seconds, then whisk in the strained stock. Continue to whisk until thickened and smooth. Check the seasoning and add a little gravy browning, if liked.

Carve the chickens and serve with the potatoes, gravy and a green vegetable alongside (see photo on pages 120–1).

THAI GREEN CURRY

My favourite Thai curry is a green curry – full of flavour and not too hot. The pastes that you can buy in small jars are fresh and very good. I like to add extra flavours, such as the lime leaves, to make this a special curry. If you can't find fresh lime leaves, jars of dried leaves are found in the spice aisle of the supermarket. Thai basil has a slightly darker leaf than Italian basil; it has more of an aniseed flavour as well, but you could use regular basil instead.

SERVES 6

2 tbsp sunflower oil

600g (1lb 5oz) skinless and boneless chicken breasts, cut into cubes

200g (7oz) button mushrooms, sliced

2 large onions, chopped

2 tsp grated fresh root ginger

2 garlic cloves, crushed

1–2 tbsp Thai green curry paste

200ml (⅓ pint) chicken stock

1 × 400g tin full-fat coconut milk

5 fresh lime leaves

1 tsp brown sugar

115g (4oz) green beans, trimmed and each sliced into 3

Juice of ½ lime

½ bunch of Thai basil, chopped

2 tbsp full-fat crème fraîche

Mary's Tips

* *Can be made up to 8 hours ahead. Blanch beans just before serving.*

Heat 1 tablespoon of the oil in a deep frying pan over a high heat. Add the chicken and fry for 5–6 minutes, until sealed but not cooked through. Using a slotted spoon, transfer to a plate and set aside.

Add the mushrooms to the pan and fry for 3 minutes until golden. Transfer to the plate with the chicken.

Add the remaining oil and the onions to the frying pan and fry for 5 minutes. Stir in the ginger, garlic and Thai paste and cook for 1 minute.

Pour in the stock and coconut milk and bring up to the boil, stirring. Add the lime leaves and sugar, and return the chicken and mushrooms to the pan, then reduce the heat and simmer for about 5 minutes.

Meanwhile, blanch the beans in boiling water for 3 minutes. Drain and add to the sauce with the lime juice, basil and crème fraîche. Stir well.

Serve hot with rice.

DOUBLE MUSTARD CHICKEN

The perfect dinner party dish, this is easy to prepare and can be made ahead.
We find some chicken breasts are too large for one serving, hence suggesting the
recipe serves 4–6. By carving each breast into thick slices, it is more attractive
on the plate and you can serve slightly less than a whole breast per person.

SERVES 4–6

4 skinless and boneless
  chicken breasts

1 tbsp runny honey

3 tbsp olive or
  sunflower oil

2 onions, thinly sliced

1 small dessert apple,
  peeled, cored and
  finely sliced

1 small piece of fresh
  root ginger, peeled
  and finely grated

2 garlic cloves, crushed

4 tbsp brandy

200ml (⅓ pint)
  chicken stock

300ml (½ pint) pouring
  double cream

3 tbsp grainy mustard

1 tbsp Dijon mustard

2 tbsp chopped flat-
  leaf parsley

Mary's Tips

* *Sauce can be made up*
  to a day ahead. Cook
  the chicken to serve.

* *Freezes well cooked.*

Season the chicken breasts with salt and freshly ground black pepper and drizzle the honey over the top.

Place a deep frying pan over a high heat until hot. Add 1 tablespoon of the oil and the chicken and fry on both sides until golden. Transfer to a plate and set aside.

Wipe the pan clean, if you need to. Add the remaining oil, the onions and apple, and cook over a medium heat for 8–10 minutes, until just tender but not coloured. Stir in the ginger and garlic and fry for a few seconds.

Pour in the brandy and reduce by half over a high heat. Pour in the stock and reduce over a high heat for a few minutes. Pour in the cream and bring up to the boil. Return the chicken to the pan, cover and reduce the heat. Simmer gently for about 10 minutes, until the chicken is cooked through.

Transfer the chicken breasts to a board to rest for 5 minutes while finishing the sauce.

Add the mustards and parsley to the pan and stir until the sauce has thickened slightly (caused by the acid in the mustards) and the sauce coats the back of a spoon.

Slice each chicken breast into three or four thick slices. Spoon the sauce over the breasts and serve with mashed potatoes and a green veg.

CHICKEN AND SPINACH HERB PARCEL

A small pastry en croûte, this is a different way to serve chicken. Perfect for sharing with a gang.

SERVES 6

4 small skinless and
  boneless chicken
  breasts, each sliced
  into 3 lengthways
2 tbsp runny honey
2 tbsp sunflower oil
1 × 320g packet of
  ready-rolled all-
  butter puff pastry
1 egg, beaten

FILLING

2 tbsp sunflower oil
1 small onion, very
  finely chopped
2 fat garlic cloves, crushed
450g (1lb) baby spinach
150g (5oz) full-fat
  cream cheese
1 tbsp chopped
  flat-leaf parsley
1 tbsp chopped
  thyme leaves
55g (2oz) Parmesan, grated
1 egg, beaten

Mary's Tips

* *Can be assembled
  and kept in the fridge
  for up to 6 hours.*
* *Freezes well cooked.*

Preheat the oven to 220°C/200°C Fan/Gas 7. Place a flat baking sheet into the oven to get hot.

To make the filling, heat the oil in a large frying pan and add the onion and garlic. Fry over a high heat for a few minutes, then cover, reduce the heat and simmer for about 10 minutes, until the onion is soft and tender. Transfer to a large bowl and leave to cool.

Season the chicken strips with salt and freshly ground black pepper and drizzle with honey. Heat the oil in the frying pan, add the chicken and brown very quickly on all sides until golden but not cooked through. Transfer to a plate to cool.

Place the spinach in a large colander and pour over a kettle of boiling water. Once the spinach is wilted, run under cold water. Drain well and squeeze out as much of the liquid as possible.

Add the spinach, cream cheese, herbs, Parmesan and beaten egg to the bowl with the onion. Season and mix well.

Lay the pastry on to a piece of floured non-stick baking paper. Roll it out to a slightly bigger rectangle (about 16 × 38cm/6¼ × 15in), with a long edge facing you. Place a third of the cold spinach filling in the middle of the rectangle vertically, making sure you leave about 1cm (½in) at the top and bottom. Top the spinach with 6 strips of chicken. Spread a third of

recipe continues overleaf…

the filling over the top, then add the final 6 strips of chicken. Cover with the remaining spinach.

Brush the edges of the pastry with beaten egg. Fold in the sides of the pastry and seal at the top and bottom.

Carefully turn the parcel over, so the join is underneath and place on a piece of non-stick baking paper. Brush the top with the remaining beaten egg and place on the preheated baking sheet and cook for about 35 minutes, until golden brown all over.

Leave to rest for about 15 minutes, then cut into thick slices and serve with a green salad or vegetables.

CHICKEN, SPINACH AND TOMATO LASAGNE

A wonderful dish for all the family. Make a couple of these when hungry teenagers are at home! I've cheated with the white sauce and made a creamy sauce for the filling instead. There are fewer layers than a traditional lasagne but it's still creamy and delicious. Soaking the lasagne sheets in water first ensures they will be cooked and tender.

SERVES 6–8

6 sheets of fresh lasagne

150g (5oz) Cheddar, grated

CHICKEN, MUSHROOM AND SPINACH MIXTURE

2 tbsp olive or sunflower oil

500g (1lb 2oz) skinless and boneless chicken thighs, diced

½ red chilli, deseeded and finely chopped

2 large garlic cloves, crushed

200g (7oz) button mushrooms, sliced

200g (7oz) baby spinach

2 tsp cornflour

200g (7oz) crème fraîche

TOMATO AND HERB SAUCE

1 tbsp chopped flat-leaf parsley

1 × 400g tin chopped tomatoes

2 tbsp sun-dried tomato paste

1 tbsp chopped thyme leaves

Preheat the oven to 200°C/180°C Fan/Gas 6. You will need a shallow 1.8 litre (3¼ pint) ovenproof dish.

To make the chicken, mushroom and spinach mixture, place the oil in a frying pan over a high heat. Add the chicken pieces and fry quickly until golden but not cooked.

Add the chilli, garlic and mushrooms and fry for a few moments. Add the spinach and stir until wilted.

Measure the cornflour into a small bowl and stir in 2 tablespoons of water until smooth.

Add the crème fraîche and parsley to the pan with the chicken and stir. Pour in the cornflour mixture and stir until thickened. Set aside.

To make the tomato and herb sauce, combine the tomatoes, sun-dried tomato paste and thyme in a bowl. Season well with salt and freshly ground black pepper and mix well.

Soak the lasagne sheets in a shallow dish filled with boiling water for a few minutes until soft.

recipe continues overleaf...

* *Can be made and
assembled up to 6
hours ahead.*

* *Freezes well uncooked.*

Spoon a third of the chicken mixture into the oven dish. Spoon a third of the tomato sauce over the chicken. Arrange three lasagne sheets on top. Repeat the layers again. Finish with a final layer of chicken mixture and tomato sauce, making three layers of chicken mixture, three layers of tomato sauce and two layers of lasagne sheets. Sprinkle the top with the grated Cheddar and bake in the preheated oven for 35–40 minutes, until golden brown and cooked through.

Serve with salad or green vegetables and the Tear and Share Cheese and Herb Rolls (see page 255) or brown bread and butter.

TUSCAN CHICKEN

Based on a classic, this is one of our favourites for an easy supper. Use chicken breasts, if you prefer.

SERVES 6

6 large skinless chicken thighs, bone in

2 tbsp plain flour

2 tsp paprika

2 tbsp olive or sunflower oil

1 large onion, finely chopped

1 large red pepper, deseeded and finely diced

2 garlic cloves, crushed

2 tsp tomato purée

30g (1oz) sun-blushed tomatoes, chopped

150ml (¼ pint) white wine

150ml (¼ pint) chicken stock

150ml (¼ pint) pouring double cream

150g (5oz) baby spinach

55g (2oz) Parmesan, grated

Mary's Tips

* *Can be made up to a day ahead.*
* *Freezes well.*

Place the chicken thighs in a bowl. Add the flour and half the paprika and season well with salt and freshly ground black pepper. Toss together to coat.

Heat the oil in a large, deep frying pan over a high heat. Add the chicken and fry for 3–4 minutes on each side, until browned and crisp. Set aside on a plate.

Add the onion and pepper to the unwashed pan and fry for 4–5 minutes over a medium heat, until soft. You may need a little more oil. Add the garlic and fry for 30 seconds.

Stir in the purée, tomatoes, wine and stock and bring up to the boil. Return the chicken to the pan with any resting juices, cover, reduce the heat and simmer for about 30 minutes, until tender.

Add the cream and spinach to the pan and stir until wilted. Remove from the heat, sprinkle with the cheese and serve piping hot.

DUCK BREAST WITH STIR-FRY VEGETABLES AND CASHEW SAUCE

Duck breasts are a favourite of mine when served pink; they are so tender and delicious. We often serve a classic French sauce alongside but this stir-fry works well.

SERVES 4

4 × 125g (4½oz) duck breasts

1 red pepper, deseeded and thinly sliced

3 thin courgettes, sliced into thin batons

1 large carrot, peeled and sliced into thin batons

1 bunch of spring onions, thinly sliced

CASHEW SAUCE

50ml (2fl oz) soy sauce

1 tbsp sesame oil

1 garlic clove

3 tbsp runny honey

55g (2oz) unsalted cashew nuts, roughly chopped

1 tsp cornflour

Mary's Tips

* Cashew sauce can be made up to a day ahead.

* Not suitable for freezing.

* Save some of the rendered duck fat in a small bowl, cover and leave to set in the fridge. Use to cook roast potatoes.

Heat a large frying pan until hot.

Score the fat of the duck and season well with salt and freshly ground black pepper.

Place the duck skin side down into the pan. Reduce the heat and cook very slowly for about 10 minutes, until the fat has rendered down and the skin is crisp. Turn the breasts over and cook for about 3 minutes for medium rare. Transfer to a warm plate and cover with foil. While the duck is resting, make the sauce.

Add all the sauce ingredients except the cornflour to a jug. Whiz with a hand blender until smooth, then pour into a small saucepan. Mix the cornflour with a little water in a bowl and stir until smooth. Pour into the saucepan and place over a medium heat. Stir until the sauce has thickened.

Meanwhile, pour off any excess duck fat from the frying pan. Add all the vegetables to the pan and stir-fry over a high heat for a 3–5 minutes, until the vegetables are just cooked, but with a crunch.

Season the vegetables and carve the duck into slices. Serve them together with the sauce.

PORK, BEEF AND LAMB

SHEPHERD'S PUFF PASTRY PIE

Think of classic shepherd's pie but with a cheat's pastry top. If your dish is deep, you may need to use a pie funnel or small teacup in the centre of the mince (put this in place before you top with pastry); this allows the steam to escape and prevents the pastry from becoming soggy.

SERVES 6

2 tbsp sunflower oil

2 large onions, roughly chopped

2 celery sticks, finely chopped

2 carrots, peeled and finely diced

1 garlic clove, crushed

1kg (2¼lb) lean minced lamb

55g (2oz) plain flour

300ml (½ pint) red wine

250ml (9fl oz) lamb or beef stock

2 tbsp Worcestershire sauce

A few drops of gravy browning

2 tbsp chopped thyme leaves

1 tbsp redcurrant jelly

250g (9oz) chestnut mushrooms, sliced

1 × 375g packet of ready-rolled all-butter puff pastry

1 egg, beaten

Mary's Tips

* Can be assembled up to 4 hours ahead.

* Freezes well uncooked.

Preheat the oven to 160°C/140°C Fan/Gas 3. You will need a 2.4 litre (4 pint) wide-based shallow ovenproof dish.

Heat 1 tablespoon of the oil in a large, deep frying pan over a medium-high heat. Add the onions, celery and carrots and fry for 5 minutes. Stir in the garlic and fry for 30 seconds. Add the lamb mince and use two spoons to break up any large lumps as it cooks. Fry for 5–6 minutes until brown.

Sprinkle over the flour and stir into the mince. Gradually blend in the red wine and stock. Bring up to the boil, stirring until thickened. Add the Worcestershire sauce, gravy browning, chopped thyme and redcurrant jelly and stir well. Transfer to the ovenproof dish, cover with foil or a lid and place in the oven for about 1 hour, until tender.

Place the mushrooms and the remaining oil in the pan and fry until the liquid has evaporated from the mushrooms. Season with salt and freshly ground black and add to the lamb mince. Set aside until cold.

Increase the oven temperature to 220°C/200°C Fan/Gas 7.

Unroll the pastry and trim to slightly bigger that the surface of the dish. Brush the inside edge of the dish (above the mince) with water. Place the pastry on top of the cold mince and press to stick the pastry to the sides of the dish. Trim and fork the edge. Score the pastry heavily in a crisscross pattern and brush the top with beaten egg. Bake in the preheated oven for 30–35 minutes until puffed up and golden brown.

LAMB AND CHICKPEA SPICED STEW

This is even better made the day before so the flavour can infuse and develop. Served with a green salad or green vegetables, it's easy to eat from a bowl, so great for a crowd. Preserved lemons are easy to buy or to preserve yourself. They are a great store-cupboard ingredient to have on hand to add zing to dishes, such as salads and dressings, in place of fresh lemon. We love them in a slow-cooked stew to give them time to infuse.

SERVES 6–8

1–2 tbsp sunflower oil

900g (2lb) lamb neck fillet or lean boneless leg of lamb or shoulder, cut into 2.5cm (1in) pieces

1 large onion, roughly chopped

2 celery sticks, finely sliced

3 fat garlic cloves, crushed

1 tsp ground ginger

1 tsp ground cinnamon

1 tbsp paprika

2 tbsp runny honey

2 × 400g tins chopped tomatoes

2 preserved lemons, finely chopped

1 × 400g tin chickpeas, rinsed and drained

Small handful of flat-leaf parsley, chopped, to garnish

Mary's Tips

* *Can be made up to a day ahead.*

* *Freezes well cooked.*

Preheat the oven to 160°C/140°C Fan/Gas 3.

Heat 1 tablespoon of the oil in a large, deep ovenproof frying pan or flameproof casserole and brown the lamb in batches. Remove with a slotted spoon and set aside.

Add another tablespoon of oil to the pan, if needed, along with the onion, celery and garlic. Stir then cover with a lid and cook over a gentle heat for 10–15 minutes, until softened.

Increase the heat and add the spices, honey, tomatoes, preserved lemons and chickpeas to the pan.

Return the browned lamb and any resting juices to the pan and bring to the boil. Season with salt and freshly ground black pepper, cover and transfer to the oven for about 1½–2 hours, until the meat is very tender.

Check the seasoning and sprinkle with chopped parsley to serve.

ROAST RACK OF LAMB WITH CELERIAC PURÉE

Rack of lamb is such a special cut of meat. Tender and delicate, it makes for a smart dish when served with this celeriac purée. The timings we've given are based on cooking a 400g (14oz) rack of lamb.

SERVES 6

2 small racks of lamb (French-trimmed)
1 tbsp sunflower oil
2 tbsp chopped thyme leaves
1 tbsp chopped flat-leaf parsley
A knob of butter
4 bay leaves

CELERIAC PURÉE

30g (1oz) butter
1 small onion, chopped
450g (1lb) celeriac, peeled and diced (peeled weight)
200ml (⅓ pint) chicken stock
115g (4oz) full-fat crème fraîche

Mary's Tips

* *The celeriac purée can be made up to 4 hours ahead. Reheat gently in a pan.*

* *Brown the lamb up to 2 hours ahead.*

* *Not suitable for freezing.*

Preheat the oven to 200°C/180°C Fan/Gas 6.

Place the lamb racks on a board. Mix the oil, thyme and parsley in a small bowl, then rub into the meat. Season well with salt and freshly ground pepper.

Place a frying pan over a high heat until hot. Add the butter and, when foaming, add the lamb and brown on both sides until just seared and golden but not cooked.

Place the bay leaves in a small roasting tin. Rest the lamb on top and roast in the oven for 15–20 minutes for medium-rare. Transfer to a warm plate, cover with foil and leave to rest for about 5–10 minutes.

Meanwhile, to make the celeriac purée, melt the butter in a saucepan over a medium heat. Add the onion and fry for a few minutes. Add the celeriac and fry for 2 minutes. Pour in the stock, season, cover with a lid and bring up to the boil. Simmer for about 15 minutes until tender.

Remove from the heat and blend until completely smooth using a hand blender. Add the crème fraîche and whiz again to combine. Check the seasoning and set aside.

Spread a pool of hot celeriac purée on a plate. Carve the lamb (between the chops) and serve on top of the celeriac with a green vegetable alongside.

SUNDAY BEST MINTED LAMB

The classic flavours of mint and redcurrant jelly are used here to make a delicious lamb stew. You could use lamb leg if you can't get neck fillet.

SERVES 6

2 tbsp sunflower oil

1.2kg (2lb 12oz) lamb neck fillet, cut into 5cm (2in) pieces

4 large banana shallots, sliced

1 leek, trimmed and sliced

2 carrots, peeled and diced

3 large garlic cloves, crushed

55g (2oz) plain flour

350ml (12fl oz) red wine

300ml (½ pint) chicken stock

1 tbsp Worcestershire sauce

2 tbsp redcurrant jelly

2 tbsp mint sauce

1 tbsp soy sauce

A large knob of butter

250g (9oz) chestnut mushrooms, halved

Mary's Tips

* *Can be made up to a day ahead. Add the mushrooms to serve.*

* *Freezes well cooked.*

Preheat the oven to 160°C/140°C Fan/Gas 3.

Heat the oil in a deep ovenproof frying pan or flameproof casserole. Fry the lamb in two batches over a high heat until browned. Remove with a slotted spoon and set aside.

Add the shallots, leek and carrots to the pan and fry for a few minutes over a high heat. Stir in the garlic and fry for 30 seconds.

Measure the flour into a bowl. Add the wine and whisk until smooth. Pour the stock and the red wine mixture into the pan with the vegetables and bring up to the boil. Stir until thickened. Add the Worcestershire sauce, redcurrant jelly and the mint and soy sauces.

Return the lamb to the pan and any resting juices, and stir. Season with salt and freshly ground black pepper, boil for a few minutes, then cover with a lid. Transfer to the oven for about 1½ hours until the lamb is tender.

Heat the butter in a small frying pan over a high heat. Add the mushrooms and fry until browned. Stir into the stew and check the seasoning.

Serve with mashed potatoes and a green vegetable.

CHIPCHIP CASSOULET

Chipolata sausages are often forgotten in favour of fat gourmet sausages, but they are perfect for this recipe as they don't release too much fat. Chipotles are dried, smoked jalapeño chillies, and chipotle chilli paste has a smoky, sweet, spicy flavour. This cassoulet is ideal for a gang of teenagers.

SERVES 6

2 tbsp sunflower oil

12 chipolata sausages

2 onions, thinly sliced

2 garlic cloves, crushed

1 red pepper, deseeded and cut into 3cm (1¼in) pieces

1 tsp chipotle paste

2 tsp sweet smoked paprika

1 tbsp tomato purée

100ml (3½fl oz) white wine

200ml (⅓ pint) chicken stock

1 x 400g tin baked beans

275g (10oz) cherry tomatoes

Mary's Tips

* Can be made up to 8 hours ahead.

* Freezes well cooked.

Heat 1 tablespoon of the oil in a deep frying pan or flameproof casserole over a high heat. Add the sausages and fry until they are evenly browned. Transfer to a plate.

Add the remaining oil to the pan, if needed. Stir in the onions, garlic and pepper and fry for a few minutes. Stir in the chipotle paste, smoked paprika and tomato purée.

Pour in the wine and stock and add the baked beans. Return the sausages to the pan, cover with a lid and bring up to the boil. Reduce the heat and simmer gently for about 25 minutes.

Add the tomatoes and return to the heat to simmer for a few minutes, until the tomatoes are soft, but still have their shape.

Serve hot with mashed or jacket potatoes.

SPICY PORK WITH SWEET POTATO AND BLACK-EYED BEANS

*A great stew to make ahead and it's perfect for sharing. You'll
just need a green vegetable to serve alongside.*

SERVES 6

2 tbsp sunflower oil

1kg (2¼lb) pork shoulder,
   cut into about 2.5cm
   (1in) pieces

2 large onions,
   thinly sliced

1 green pepper,
   deseeded and diced

2 large garlic cloves,
   crushed

½–1 red chilli, deseeded
   and finely chopped

1 tbsp each ground
   cumin, ground
   coriander and paprika

2 x 400g tins chopped
   tomatoes

200ml (⅓ pint)
   chicken stock

2 tbsp tomato purée

2 tsp caster sugar

1 x 400g tin black-eyed
   beans, rinsed and drained

1 large sweet potato,
   peeled and cut into
   2cm (¾in) cubes

Mary's Tips

* *Can be partly made
   up to 2 days ahead.
   Add the beans and
   sweet potato and finish
   cooking when reheating.*

* *Freezes well without the
   beans and sweet potato.*

Preheat the oven to 160°C/140°C Fan/Gas 3.

Heat the oil in a large ovenproof frying pan or
flameproof casserole over a high heat. Add the pork
and fry in batches for 3–4 minutes, until sealed and
browned. Remove with a slotted spoon and set aside.

Add the onions and pepper to the pan and fry for
5 minutes, until softened. Add the garlic, chilli and
spices and fry for a few seconds, then stir in the
tomatoes, stock, purée and sugar.

Return the pork and any resting juices to the pan
and season with salt and freshly ground black pepper.
Bring up to the boil, stirring, then cover with a lid and
transfer to the oven for about 1 hour.

Add the rinsed beans and the sweet potato to the stew
and return to the oven for 30–45 minutes, or until the
pork is tender and the potatoes are cooked.

LOIN OF STUFFED PORK WITH CRACKLING AND WHITE WINE GRAVY

This is a pork loin stuffed with a superb green filling but, as the loin is hollowed out, you don't have the difficulty of tying up and removing string at the end. I've added a new way to make foolproof crackling. Slicing the fat into strips before cooking ensures everyone will be able to have some crackling and there's no messy cutting at the end.

SERVES 6

1.7kg (3½lb) boned loin of pork, skin scored

STUFFING

A knob of butter

1 small onion, finely chopped

2 garlic cloves, crushed

1–2 pork sausages

3 heaped tbsp chopped flat-leaf parsley

1 tbsp chopped thyme leaves

GRAVY

100ml (3½fl oz) white wine

450ml (¾ pint) good-quality stock

3 tbsp plain flour

A dash of Worcestershire sauce

1 tbsp apple sauce from a jar

Gravy browning (optional)

Preheat the oven to 200°C/180°C Fan/Gas 6 and line a large, deep roasting tin with non-stick baking paper.

First make the stuffing. Melt the butter in a large frying pan over a medium heat. Add the onion and garlic and fry for 2–3 minutes. Lower the heat, cover with a lid and simmer for about 10 minutes, stirring occasionally, until softened. Season with salt and freshly ground black pepper and set aside until cold.

Remove the sausage meat from the skin and add the meat to the cold onion. Sprinkle in the parsley and thyme, season and mix well (it is easiest to do this with your hands).

Remove the scored skin and a thin layer of fat from the pork using a very sharp knife (leaving a good layer of fat over the whole joint). Snip the skin into strips with kitchen scissors.

Place the pork on the worktop fat side down, make a deep incision through the eye of the lean pork loin with a sharp knife, turning it to make a tunnel. Fill the tunnel with the stuffing, packing it in with your fingers from either end.

recipe continues overleaf...

Place the joint on one side of the lined roasting tin and the strips of skin on the other. Sprinkle everything with salt and roast in the oven for about 1¼–1½ hours until the juices run clear. The thin strips of crackling should be golden and crisp. Transfer the pork to a serving plate, cover with foil and leave to rest.

Carefully pour the fat from the roasting tin into a small bowl. Remove the baking paper and discard.

Pour the wine and stock into the roasting tin and place over a high heat. Bring up to the boil.

Meanwhile, measure 3 tablespoons of pork fat from the bowl into a medium saucepan and all the flour. Whisk over a medium heat for a few seconds. Carefully pour the hot stock and wine into the saucepan, whisking all the time, until the gravy has boiled and thickened. Add the Worcestershire sauce, apple sauce and gravy browning, if using, and pour the gravy into a warm jug.

Carve the pork and serve with the crackling and gravy.

BEEF BOURGUIGNON PIE

*Beef Bourguignon, the classic French beef stew with red wine, is famous.
Adding a pastry top makes it extra special an substantional. If you have a pie
funnel, sit it in the centre of the meat, before adding the pastry – this allows the steam
to release, preventing the pastry from going soggy. It's old-fashioned but very useful!
As not everyone has a pie funnel, we've suggested making a cross in the centre of the
pastry here instead.*

SERVES 6

600ml (1 pint) red wine

2 tbsp sunflower oil

800g (1lb 12oz) braising beef, cut into 4cm (1½in) cubes

200g (7oz) smoked diced bacon lardons

500g (1lb 2oz) baby shallots, peeled but kept whole

3 garlic cloves, crushed

400g (14oz) button mushrooms

55g (2oz) plain flour

150ml (¼ pint) cold beef stock

1 tbsp tomato purée

2 tbsp chopped thyme leaves

3 bay leaves

1 tbsp redcurrant jelly

1 × 500g block of all-butter puff pastry

1 egg, beaten

You will need a 2 litre (3½ pint) ovenproof dish, ideally with a lip.

Pour the wine into a saucepan. Bring to the boil and reduce by a third (to give 400ml/14fl oz). This gives a more intense flavour.

Meanwhile, heat the oil in a large, deep ovenproof frying pan or flameproof casserole over a high heat. Add the beef and brown in batches. Remove with a slotted spoon and set aside.

Add the bacon and shallots to the pan and fry over a high heat for a 3–4 minutes, until brown. Stir in the garlic and mushrooms and fry for few minutes.

Measure the flour into a bowl. Pour in the cold stock and whisk until smooth. Add the stock and reduced wine to the pan and bring up to the boil, whisking until thickened. Stir in the purée, thyme, bay and jelly.

Return the beef and any resting juices to the pan and bring to the boil. Cover with a lid and cook in the oven for about 2½ hours until tender.

Transfer the stew to the ovenproof dish, remove the bay leaf and set aside to cool. Chill in the fridge.

Preheat the oven to 160°C/140°C Fan/Gas 3.

recipe continues overleaf...

Mary's Tips

* *Can be made up to
  5 hours ahead.*
* *Freezes well uncooked*

Roll out the pastry on a floured work surface to about 5cm (2in) bigger than the ovenproof dish. Trim a strip from the edges. Wet the lip or edge of the dish with water, then stick the pastry strips on top. Brush the strips with beaten egg, then carefully lift the sheet of pastry over the filling. Press down around the edges to seal. (If your dish is deep, you may need to use a pie funnel or small teacup in the centre of the meat – put this in place before you top with pastry. Lift the pastry over the top and poke the pie funnel through the centre.)

Trim, crimp and flute the edges of the pastry. If you don't have a pie funnel, use a sharp knife to make a little cross in the centre of the pie. Brush the top with beaten egg and decorate with any trimmings.

Increase the oven temperate to 220°C/200°C Fan/Gas 7 and bake the pie for 35–40 minutes, until golden brown on top and hot in the middle.

Serve with vegetables.

BLACK BEAN BEEF NOODLE STIR-FRY

Choose sirloin, rump or fillet steak for this recipe. Sliced thinly and cooked quickly, it will be tender. Find black bean sauce in the Asian section of the supermarket.

SERVES 4-6

3 tbsp sunflower oil

350g (12oz) sirloin or rump steak, sliced into very thin strips

120g (4¼oz) medium egg noodles

3 large banana shallots, sliced

1 red pepper, deseeded and thinly sliced

200g (7oz) closed-cup mushrooms, halved or quartered if large

5 spring onions, sliced

SAUCE

100ml (3½fl oz) black bean sauce

½ tsp sesame oil

2 tbsp soy sauce

2 garlic cloves, crushed

1 tsp grated fresh root ginger

Mary's Tips

* Best made and served immediately.
* Not suitable for freezing.

Measure the sauce ingredients into a bowl and mix to combine.

Heat the oil in a large frying pan over a high heat. When the oil is very hot, add the steak and fry quickly until golden, but still pink. Using a slotted spoon, transfer to a plate.

Meanwhile, cook the noodles in boiling water according to the packet instructions. Drain and set aside.

Place the shallots, pepper and mushrooms in the pan and fry for a few minutes. Add the cooked noodles and pour in the sauce. Toss over the heat.

Return the beef to the pan and season with freshly ground black pepper. Spoon into bowls and sprinkle with spring onions to serve.

STICKY SHORT BEEF RIBS
AND LEMON COLESLAW

*These short ribs are readily available and a great and different way to serve
slow-cooked beef. They do take a long time, so plan ahead. Use red cabbage
in the coleslaw but, if preferred, try finely shredded white cabbage.*

SERVES 6

1.5kg (3lb 5oz) beef
 short ribs

MARINADE

100ml (3½fl oz) ketchup

75ml (2½fl oz) apple juice

2 tbsp Worcestershire
 sauce

1 tbsp white wine vinegar

4 tbsp maple syrup

2 tbsp soy sauce

4 garlic cloves, crushed

A good pinch of
 dried chilli flakes

COLESLAW

8 tbsp mayonnaise

Juice of ½ lemon

1 tbsp Dijon mustard

½ garlic clove, crushed

½ red cabbage,
 finely shredded

2 large carrots, peeled
 and coarsely grated

2 celery sticks, finely sliced

2 spring onions,
 finely sliced

To make the marinade, measure all the ingredients
into a shallow dish and mix well. Add the shorts ribs
and toss to coat. Leave for 2 hours or overnight in the
fridge, if possible, to marinate.

Preheat the oven to 150°C/130°C Fan/Gas 2.

Transfer the ribs and the marinade into a deep
ovenproof saucepan or flameproof casserole. Add 200ml
(⅓ pint) water so only the bones are sticking above the
liquid. Cover with a lid and bring up to the boil.

Transfer to the oven for about 3½ hours, or until the
ribs are tender. Remove from the oven and leave to
cool in the pan for about 1 hour.

Line a small roasting tin with non-stick baking paper.
Remove the ribs from the marinade, give them a shake
and sit on the paper in the tin.

Skim the fat from the marinade in the pan and
discard. Heat the marinade over a high heat and
reduce the liquid by half. Pour the sauce over the ribs
in the tin.

Increase the oven temperature to 200°C/180°C Fan/
Gas 6 and roast the ribs for about 15 minutes until
dark brown and sticky.

* *Cook the ribs in the pan up to 8 hours ahead. Roast in the oven to become sticky to serve.*

* *Coleslaw can be made up to a day ahead.*

* *Not suitable for freezing.*

Meanwhile, to make the coleslaw, measure the mayonnaise, lemon juice, mustard and garlic into a large bowl. Mix and season well with salt and freshly ground black pepper.

Add the cabbage, carrots, celery and spring onions and toss to coat everything well. Spoon into a serving bowl.

Serve the sticky ribs in a bowl alongside the coleslaw with jacket potatoes and corn on the cob (see photo on pages 160–1).

FILLET STEAK FOR TWO WITH GREEN PEPPERCORN AND BRANDY SAUCE

Sharing is not just for a party. The best and most special of sharing moments can be for two, so this fillet steak recipe is as much about the food as it is about the time spent together. Green peppercorns are soft peppercorns in brine, sold in a jar or a can. If preferred, you could use crushed black peppercorns.

SERVES 2

2 × 150g (5oz) centre cut fillet steaks

30g (1oz) butter

SAUCE

2 banana shallots, finely chopped

3 tbsp brandy

2 tsp Dijon mustard

A good dash of Worcestershire sauce

100ml (3½fl oz) pouring double cream

1 tsp green peppercorns, crushed

1 tbsp chopped flat-leaf parsley

Mary's Tips

* *The sauce can be made up to 12 hours ahead.*

* *Not suitable for freezing.*

* *Buy fillets of an equal size and shape so they cook at the same rate.*

Beat out the steaks using the palm of your hand to about 1.5cm (⅔in) thick. Season well with salt and freshly ground black pepper.

Heat a large frying pan over a high heat until hot. Add half the butter and, as it sizzles, add the steaks to the pan. Fry for 1½ minutes on each side for medium rare. Transfer to a plate, cover with foil and keep warm.

Add the remaining butter and the shallots to the pan and cook for 3–4 minutes over a low heat until softened.

Pour in the brandy and bubble for a moment. Stir in the mustard, Worcestershire sauce and cream, bring to the boil, season with salt and add the green peppercorns. The sauce should be the consistency of pouring cream; if it is a bit thick, add a little water. Taste and add more peppercorns, if liked.

Add the parsley and any resting juices to the sauce and serve with the fillet steak.

VEGGIE MAINS

VEGETABLE PAD THAI

Commonly served as street food in Thailand, this noodle dish is very popular in the West, too. Tamarind paste is a sweet and sour paste made from the tamarind fruit. It is more traditional to serve this without the omelette. Or you could fry an egg and serve that on top of each portion, if you wish.

SERVES 4

3 tbsp sunflower oil

3 eggs, beaten

200g (7oz) flat rice noodles

1 large carrot, peeled and sliced into matchsticks

1 red pepper, deseeded and thinly sliced

3 large banana shallots, sliced

½ red chilli, deseeded and finely chopped

Small bunch of coriander, roughly chopped

115g (4oz) fresh bean sprouts

75g (3oz) salted peanuts, chopped

SAUCE

2 tbsp soy sauce

3 tbsp fish sauce

2 tbsp light muscovado sugar

2 tsp tamarind paste

3 garlic cloves, crushed

2 tbsp sweet chilli sauce

Juice of 1 large lime

Mary's Tips

* Prep the ingredients and cook to serve.

* Not suitable for freezing.

Mix all the sauce ingredients together in a small bowl and set aside.

Heat a large frying pan or wok over a medium-high heat. Add 1 tablespoon of the oil and the eggs and swirl them around the pan to make a thin flat omelette. Cook for 2–3 minutes until set, then flip over and cook for another minute. Transfer to a board and slice into very thin strips.

Cook the noodles in boiling water according to the packet instructions. Drain and refresh under cold water. Drain again.

Heat the remaining oil in the large frying pan over a high heat. Add the carrot, pepper and shallots and fry for 4–5 minutes. Add the chilli and fry for 30 seconds. Add the cooked noodles and toss everything together.

Pour in the sauce, season with freshly ground black pepper and toss over the heat quickly until well mixed and heated through.

Add the coriander, bean sprouts, peanuts and strips of omelette and serve at once.

CELERY, BLUE CHEESE AND SAGE RISOTTO

A complete midweek meal, prepared and cooked in under three-quarters of an hour.
You can use any blue cheese you have leftover or choose the one you like best.

SERVES 4

2 tbsp olive or
 sunflower oil
2 onions, finely chopped
5 celery sticks, diced
2 garlic cloves, crushed
200g (7oz) small chestnut
 mushrooms, sliced
275g (10oz) risotto rice
250ml (9fl oz) white wine
750ml (1⅓ pints) hot
 vegetable stock
150g (5oz) frozen
 petits pois
115g (4oz) blue cheese,
 e.g. Stilton or dolcelatte,
 coarsely grated
2 tbsp chopped sage,
 plus a few extra
 leaves to garnish
A knob of butter

Mary's Tips

* *Best made and served.*
* *Not suitable for freezing.*

Heat the oil in a deep frying pan over a high heat. Add the onions and celery and fry for 4–5 minutes, to soften. Add the garlic and mushrooms and fry for a further 2–3 minutes. Add the rice and stir into the vegetables.

Pour in the wine and let it bubble for 1–2 minutes until reduced. Add a ladleful of the hot stock and continue to add all the stock, a little at a time, until the liquid has absorbed. This will take about 15–20 minutes.

Add the petits pois and cook for a few minutes. Turn off the heat and stir in the cheese and sage. Season with a little salt and plenty of ground black pepper. Leave to stand for 2 minutes until the cheese has melted.

Melt the butter in a small pan over a high heat and fry a few sage leaves until crisp.

Serve the risotto hot in warm bowls with the crispy sage leaves to garnish.

PROVENCE TOMATO AND GARLIC PISTOU TART

With thin cheesy pastry and juicy roasted tomatoes, this is the perfect tart for sharing on lazy sunny days with a glass of rosé and memories of French holidays! Pistou is a French garlic and basil sauce, similar to Italian pesto. In Provence there is also a traditional soupe au pistou *which uses the same flavours.*

SERVES 6-8

CHEESE PASTRY

175g (6oz) plain flour, plus extra for dusting

115g (4oz) butter, cubed

55g (2oz) Parmesan, grated

1 egg, beaten

FILLING

1kg (2¼lb) medium-sized ripe tomatoes, thickly sliced

4 tbsp olive oil

5 garlic cloves, halved

3 tbsp sun-dried tomato paste

115g (4oz) Brie, cut into thin slices

PISTOU

2 garlic cloves

2 tsp sea salt

Small bunch of basil (15g/½oz)

Small bunch of mint, leaves picked (15g/½oz)

75ml (2½fl oz) olive oil

A squeeze of fresh lemon juice

Preheat the oven to 200°C/180°C Fan/Gas 6. You will need a 33 × 23cm (13 × 9in) Swiss roll tin.

To make the pastry, measure the flour, butter and Parmesan into a food processor. Whiz until breadcrumb stage. Add the egg and ½ tablespoon of water and whiz again until the mixture comes together. Tip out on to a floured work surface and knead gently into a ball. Roll the pastry out thinly and use it to line the base and sides of the tin. Prick the base with a fork and chill in the fridge for 30 minutes.

Arrange the tomatoes in a single layer in a large roasting tin.

Place the oil and garlic in a small bowl. Swirl around to coat the garlic in the oil, then pour the oil over the tomatoes. Tuck the cloves between the sliced tomatoes and season well with salt and freshly ground black pepper.

Line the pastry with non-stick baking paper and fill with baking beans. Slide on to the middle shelf of the oven. Place the tomatoes on the top shelf and cook both for 20 minutes. Take the pastry case out of the oven and remove the paper and beans. Return the pastry to the oven with the tomatoes for another 5–10 minutes, until the pastry case has dried out and the tomatoes are soft but not mushy. Leave them both to cool slightly in the tins.

* *It is important to use a large roasting tin for the tomatoes, so they are not piled on top of each other. Having enough space in the tin allows the liquid to evaporate.*

* *Can be made up to 8 hours ahead and warmed to serve. Pistou can be made up to 2 days ahead.*

* *Not suitable for freezing.*

Spread the sun-dried tomato paste over the base of the pastry, then carefully arrange the roasted tomatoes in neat rows on top, making sure not to add too much of the juice from the roasting tin. Scatter the garlic cloves over the top and season again. Return to the oven for 10-15 minutes, until the tomatoes are lightly tinged.

Meanwhile, to make the pistou, place the garlic, salt and herbs in a food processor and whiz. While the processor is still whizzing, slowly pour in the olive oil to make a soft paste. Add a splash of lemon juice.

Lay the slices of Brie over the warm tart and return to the oven for 3–4 minutes to melt a little.

Drizzle over the pistou and serve warm with a dressed green salad (see photo on pages 172–3).

PORCINI, WILD MUSHROOM AND WATERCRESS GRATIN

I am not a huge fan of kale, but I have been persuaded to use it as I know
it is loved by many. I think young kale has the best flavour but you could
use shredded kale instead. Serve in small portions, as it is rich.

SERVES 4

30g (1oz) dried porcini
   mushrooms
300ml (½ pint)
   boiling water
5 tbsp olive oil
55g (2oz) butter, plus
   2 knobs for frying
350g (12oz) oyster
   mushrooms,
   thickly sliced
200g (7oz) button
   mushrooms, sliced
2 large garlic cloves,
   crushed
115g (4oz) young kale,
   thickly sliced
150g (5oz) watercress
55g (2oz) plain flour
400ml (14fl oz) milk
2 tbsp pouring
   double cream
115g (4oz) Parmesan,
   grated

Mary's Tips

* *Can be assembled*
  up to 5 hours ahead,
  ready to cook.
* *Not suitable for freezing.*

Preheat the oven to 200°C/180°C Fan/Gas 6.

Place the dried porcini mushrooms in a jug. Add the boiling water and leave to soak for 30 minutes.

Place a large pan over a medium-high heat. Add 2 tablespoons of the oil, a knob of butter, half the mushrooms and half the garlic. Toss over the heat for 1–2 minutes, then cover with a lid and cook for 1 minute to release the liquid. Remove the lid and fry for 1 minute, until the mushrooms have softened. Transfer to a plate and repeat with the remaining mushrooms and garlic.

Place ½ tablespoon of oil in the pan over a medium heat. Add the kale and fry until wilted. Transfer to a plate and repeat the process with the watercress.

Strain the dried mushrooms, reserving the liquid, and roughly chop. Add to the other mushrooms and season.

Melt the 55g (2oz) butter in a saucepan over a medium heat. Add the flour and stir for a few seconds. Whisk in 200ml (⅓ pint) of the reserved porcini liquid and all the milk until thickened. Add the cream, half the cheese and season.

Spread half the mushrooms, half the kale and half the watercress over the base of an ovenproof dish. Mix the remaining vegetables with the sauce and pour over the top. Sprinkle with the remaining cheese and bake for about 25 minutes, until golden and bubbling around the edges.

SPAGHETTI WITH PEAS AND PESTO

A quick and easy midweek pasta dish. Adding peas to the pesto gives a lovely natural fresh flavour. Use fresh garden peas, if you grow them, instead of petits pois. We have used cashew nuts instead of pine nuts in the pesto to give creaminess to the sauce.

SERVES 4–6

350g (12oz) spaghetti

PEA PESTO

250g (9oz) frozen petits pois

115g (4oz) unsalted cashew nuts

55g (2oz) Parmesan, grated, plus extra to serve (optional)

2 large garlic cloves, halved

Large bunch of basil, roughly chopped

100ml (3½fl oz) olive oil

Mary's Tips

* Best made and served. The pea pesto can be made up to 6 hours ahead.

* Not suitable for freezing.

Cook the peas in a saucepan of boiling water for 3 minutes. Drain and refresh under cold water. Drain again.

Place half the peas in a small food processor and add the nuts, cheese, garlic and basil. Whiz until finely chopped. Slowly add the oil, a little a time, until you have a paste consistency. Season with salt to taste.

Cook the spaghetti in boiling salted water according to the packet instructions. Reserve 50ml (2fl oz) of the pasta water before draining.

Place the pesto in a large non-stick frying pan, add the reserved peas and the cooked spaghetti and a little of the pasta water. Toss everything over a high heat until well coated.

Season well with freshly ground black pepper and serve with extra Parmesan, if liked.

FIVE VEG PASTA

Served in a large dish, this is full of colour. If you like chilli, add
one finely chopped red chilli for a little kick. Sit the bowl in the
centre of the table and let everyone serve themselves.

SERVES 6

225g (8oz) penne

6 tbsp olive oil

1 medium courgette,
  sliced into thin batons

2 large red peppers,
  deseeded and
  thinly sliced

2 onions, finely sliced

3 garlic cloves, crushed

200g (7oz) button
  mushrooms, finely sliced

200g (7oz) sugar snap
  peas, halved lengthways

Small bunch of
  basil, chopped

75g (3oz) Parmesan, grated

Mary's Tips

* *Best made and
  served at once.*

* *Not suitable for freezing.*

Cook the pasta in boiling salted water according to
the packet instructions. Drain well.

Heat a tablespoon of the oil in a large deep sauté
pan over a high heat. Add the courgette and peppers
and fry for a few minutes until starting to soften and
brown. Remove with a slotted spoon and set aside.

Add 2 tablespoons of the oil and the onions to the pan
and fry for a few minutes until almost soft. Add the
garlic, mushrooms and sugar snap peas and stir-fry
over a high heat for 3–4 minutes, until softening but
still crisp.

Add the drained pasta, the remaining oil and the
courgette and peppers to the pan. Season well with
salt and freshly ground black pepper, and scatter
in the basil and Parmesan. Toss over the heat until
piping hot.

Tip into a large bowl and serve.

GARDENER'S STUFFED SQUASH

Very popular in South Africa and easy to grow here, the lovely, round, mini acorn or gem squash are perfect for this dish. If you can't find mini squash, you could also use the round end of a butternut and save the narrow end to use another day. The courgette, mushroom and tomato stuffing makes this hearty and full of flavour, and if you are a keen gardener, are veg you might have grown at home. Serve one or two halves each.

SERVES 4–8

4 round mini squash, e.g. small acorn or gem squash

2 tbsp olive or sunflower oil

1 courgette, finely diced

200g (7oz) chestnut mushrooms, finely chopped

1 large garlic clove, crushed

Finely grated zest of 1 small lemon

1 tbsp chopped mint leaves

3 medium tomatoes, deseeded and chopped

115g (4oz) feta, crumbled

55g (2oz) Parmesan, coarsely grated

Mary's Tips

* *Can be assembled up to 6 hours ahead.*

* *Not suitable for freezing.*

Preheat the oven to 200°C/180°C Fan/Gas 6 and grease a large roasting tin.

Slice a thin sliver from the base and top of each squash (so they stand upright when halved) and cut each squash in half horizontally. Scoop out the seeds. Bring a large saucepan of water to the boil, add the squashes so they are submerged and boil for 8 minutes, until just tender. Drain well and place the squashes flesh side up in the prepared tin.

Meanwhile, to make the filling, heat the oil in a frying pan over a high heat. Add the courgette and mushrooms and fry for 4–5 minutes, until browned. Add the garlic, lemon zest, mint and tomatoes and fry for another minute. Season with salt and freshly ground black pepper and spoon into a bowl. Leave to cool slightly.

Add the feta to the courgette mixture and mix well. Divide between the squash halves and sprinkle each squash with Parmesan. Bake in the preheated oven for 25–30 minutes, until the cheese is golden and the squash is tender.

CURRIED SQUASH AND PANEER FILO SAMOSAS

The authentic way to cook a samosa is to deep-fry, but I prefer to bake them in the oven and use filo pastry – a Western twist!

MAKES 25

- 2 tbsp olive or sunflower oil
- 1 large onion, roughly chopped
- 500g (1lb 2oz) butternut squash, peeled and chopped into 1.5cm (⅔in) cubes (peeled weight)
- 2 tsp grated fresh root ginger
- 2 tsp mild curry powder
- 1 tbsp garam masala
- 1 tbsp mango chutney
- A squeeze of fresh lemon juice
- 115g (4oz) paneer cheese, cut into small cubes
- 2 tbsp chopped coriander
- 1 × 270g packet of filo pastry (about 5 sheets, each 46 × 26cm/18 ×10½in)
- 55g (2oz) butter, melted

Mary's Tips

* *Can be made up to 8 hours ahead. Cook to serve.*

* *Freeze well uncooked.*

Heat the oil in a large frying pan. Add the onion and squash and fry over a medium heat for about 10 minutes, until the vegetables are softened. Add the ginger and spices and fry for another 2 minutes.

Spoon the vegetables into a bowl, add the mango chutney, lemon juice, paneer cheese and coriander and mix together. Season well with salt and freshly ground black pepper and leave to cool.

Preheat the oven to 200°C/180°C Fan/Gas 6 and line a baking sheet with non-stick baking paper.

Place one sheet of filo pastry on a work surface. Brush with melted butter. Divide the sheet into 5 equal strips measuring about 9 × 26cm (3½ ×10½in). Put one heaped tablespoon of filling at the top of one strip. Fold over to make a triangle and continue to fold until you reach the bottom of the pastry strip. Continue with the remaining sheets of filo and filling, to make 25 samosas.

Arrange the samosas on the prepared baking sheet and brush with a little butter. Cook in the oven for 20–25 minutes, until golden brown and crisp.

Serve hot with a chutney of your choice.

SABZI VEGETABLE CURRY

*A hearty, tomato-based North Indian-style dry curry full of vegetables and
bursting with flavour. You can adapt the recipe to your preference – double up
on some veg and leave others out, as long as they have a similar weight.*

SERVES 6

2 tbsp sunflower oil

2 onions, sliced

3 garlic cloves, crushed

1 small green chilli,
deseeded and
finely chopped

4cm (1½in) piece of
fresh root ginger,
peeled and grated

1 tbsp garam marsala

1 tbsp medium
curry powder

1 tsp each ground cumin
and ground turmeric

225g (8oz) small new
potatoes, halved or
quartered if large

1 large aubergine, cut
into large cubes

1 red pepper, deseeded
and finely diced

1 large carrot, peeled
and finely diced

2 celery sticks, finely sliced

300ml (½ pint)
vegetable stock

1 x 400g tin chopped
tomatoes

2–3 tbsp mango chutney

75g (3oz) frozen petits pois

Mary's Tips

* Can be made up to
  2 days ahead.

* Freezes well without peas.

Heat the oil in a large, deep frying pan over a
medium-high heat. Add the onions and fry for
2–3 minutes. Add the garlic, chilli, ginger and spices
and fry for 1–2 minutes. Add the potatoes, aubergine,
pepper, carrot and celery and coat in the mixture.

Pour the stock and add the tomatoes into the pan, stir
and bring to the boil. Cover with a lid, reduce the heat
and simmer for about 30 minutes, until the potatoes
are tender.

Stir in the mango chutney and season well with salt
and freshly ground black pepper. Add the peas and
cook for a few minutes.

Serve hot with basmati rice.

MAJORCAN-STYLE ONE POT VEGETABLES

A rustic dish of layered of potatoes, aubergines and peppers. Double up the recipe if there's a crowd. This is good to cook ahead as it reheats well.

SERVES 6

2 large aubergines, sliced into rounds about 2cm (¾in) thick

Olive oil, for cooking and drizzling

3 red peppers, deseeded and cut into pieces

700g (1lb 9oz) potatoes, peeled and cut into cubes

2 tsp ground cumin

2 onions, finely chopped

½–1 red chilli, deseeded and finely chopped

2 large garlic cloves, crushed

2 × 400g tin chopped tomatoes

1 tbsp tomato purée

A dash of sugar

Small bunch of coriander, chopped (optional)

Mary's Tips

* *Can be made a day ahead and reheated. Add the chopped coriander to serve.*

* *Not suitable for freezing.*

Preheat the oven to 220°C/200°C Fan/Gas 7 and line two large baking sheets with non-stick baking paper.

Place the slices of aubergine on one of the baking sheets in a single layer. Brush both sizes with olive oil and season with salt and freshly ground black pepper. Place the peppers in one half of the second baking sheet and the potatoes on the other side. Drizzle both with oil and season. Place both baking sheets in the oven and roast for 30 minutes, until the vegetables are soft and tinged brown. Sprinkle the ground cumin over the potatoes and toss lightly together.

Reduce the temperature to 200°C/180°C Fan/Gas 6.

Heat 2 tablespoons of oil in a large saucepan over a high heat. Add the onions and fry for 3–4 minutes. Add the chilli and garlic and fry for a few seconds. Add the chopped tomatoes, purée and sugar and bring to the boil. Cover with a lid, reduce the heat and simmer for about 10 minutes. Season well.

Place half the potatoes in the base of an ovenproof dish. Scatter over the peppers and arrange a neat row of aubergines on top. Spoon half the tomato sauce over the vegetables and sprinkle with half the coriander, if using. Repeat with a second layer of potatoes, peppers and aubergines, finishing with a layer of tomato sauce. Cover with foil and bake in the preheated oven for about 30 minutes.

Remove the foil and sprinkle with the remaining coriander, if using, to serve.

CAULIFLOWER POTATO CAKES
WITH PARMESAN SAUCE

I just love anything with cauliflower, so adding it to a potato cake makes perfect sense to me! You must use full-fat crème fraîche, as reduced fat will give too thin a sauce.

MAKES 8

500g (1lb 2oz) potatoes,
  peeled and cubed

500g (1lb 2oz) cauliflower,
  chopped into florets

2 tsp Dijon mustard

115g (4oz) mature
  Cheddar, grated

2 tbsp chopped chives

6 spring onions,
  finely chopped

2 tbsp mayonnaise

75g (3oz) panko
  breadcrumbs

Sunflower oil, for frying

PARMESAN SAUCE

200g (7oz) full-fat
  crème fraîche

55g (2oz) Parmesan, grated

2 tsp grainy mustard

2 tsp chopped chives

Mary's Tips

* *Can be made up to
  8 hours ahead.*

* *Not suitable for freezing.*

Place the potatoes in a saucepan of cold salted water. Cover with a lid and bring up to the boil. Boil for 10–15 minutes until tender. Drain well and mash.

Boil the cauliflower in salted water for 3 minutes. Drain and refresh under cold water. Drain again. Roughly chop into small pieces and set aside until cool enough to handle.

Mix the mustard, Cheddar, chives, spring onions, mayonnaise and 30g (1oz) of the breadcrumbs together in a bowl. Season well with salt and freshly ground black pepper. Stir in the potato and cauliflower. Shape into 8 cakes (like fishcakes). Coat each one in the remaining breadcrumbs and chill in the fridge for about 30 minutes before frying.

Meanwhile, make the sauce. Measure the crème fraîche into a saucepan and bring to the boil. Remove from the heat, add the cheese and mustard and stir until melted. Season well and stir in the chives.

Heat a little oil in a frying pan over a high heat. Add the cauliflower potato cakes and fry for 3–4 minutes on each side until golden and crispy.

Serve hot with the sauce.

SALADS
AND SIDES

CORONATION COLESLAW

*The lovely mild curry flavours of coronation chicken are used here as a sauce
for coleslaw. We think it works really well and is great for sharing or a party.
Traditionally, you'd use apricot jam, but mango chutney adds a first-class twist.*

SERVES 4–6

500g (1lb 2oz) white
  cabbage, very
  finely shredded

3 carrots, peeled and
  coarsely grated or
  thinly sliced into very
  thin matchstick strips

1 small onion, very
  thinly sliced

300g (10½oz) celeriac,
  peeled and thinly
  sliced into very thin
  matchstick strips

3 celery sticks,
  thinly sliced

CORONATION SAUCE

8 tbsp mayonnaise

150ml (¼ pint)
  soured cream

2 tbsp mild curry powder

3 tbsp mango chutney

Juice of 1 lemon

Small bunch of
  coriander or flat-leaf
  parsley, chopped

Mary's Tips

* *Keep up to 3 days
  in the fridge.*
* *Not suitable for freezing.*
* *For speed, use a food
  processor for chopping
  and slicing the vegetables.*

Measure all the sauce ingredients into a large bowl
and season with salt and freshly ground black pepper.
Mix together to combine.

Place all the prepared vegetables in the bowl with the
sauce and fold everything together until well coated.
Cover with cling film and chill in the fridge for 1 hour
before serving.

GREEK SALAD WITH ASPARAGUS

The choice of tomatoes available to us is wide, so choose different colours and flavours to make this a little different.

SERVES 4–6

8 asparagus spears
1 cucumber, peeled
270g (10oz) cherry tomatoes (use a variety of colours and types), halved
150g (5oz) feta, crumbled
70g (2½oz) pitted good-quality whole black olives
1 tbsp capers, drained
Handful of mint leaves, left whole or roughly torn
Juice of ½ lemon
4 tbsp olive oil

Mary's Tips

* Can be assembled up to 2 hours ahead. Dress and season to serve.

Remove the woody ends from the asparagus. Cut each spear in half. Bring a pan of salted water to the boil, add the asparagus and cook for 3 minutes. Drain and refresh in cold water. Drain again.

Slice the cucumber in half lengthways and remove the seeds with a teaspoon. Slice into crescents and place in a serving bowl. Add the tomatoes, feta, olives, capers, asparagus pieces and mint leaves. Toss everything together gently.

Drizzle with the lemon juice and olive oil, and season with sea salt and freshly ground black pepper to serve.

NOODLE NORI SALAD

This salad is perfect with the sushi platters on pages 78–81 or on its own or with cold meats. If you can't get soba noodles, use bean thread noodles (these are very fine and opaque when cooked) or rice noodles. Nori is the Japanese word for seaweed, and it can be bought in flat sheets in all good supermarkets. Daikon are Japanese white radishes. If you can't find any, use the common British red ones. All the vegetables should be sliced very, very thinly for a delicate salad.

SERVES 4–6

125g (4½oz) soba noodles

1 sheet nori (seaweed), finely shredded

2 daikon (or 5 red radishes), finely sliced

2 spring onions, finely sliced on the diagonal

1 small red pepper, deseeded and finely sliced into thin strips

1 large carrot, peeled and coarsely grated

1 celery stick, finely sliced

1 tbsp chopped flat-leaf parsley

DRESSING

2 tbsp pickled ginger, finely chopped

4 tbsp rice wine vinegar

2 tbsp soy sauce

2 tbsp olive oil

Mary's Tips

* *Can be made up to 4 hours ahead. Dress to serve.*

* *Not suitable for freezing.*

Cook the noodles according to the packet instructions. Drain and refresh in cold water. Drain again and set aside to cool.

Measure all the dressing ingredients into a small bowl or jug and mix together to combine.

Place the cold noodles, all the vegetables and the parsley in a large bowl. Season with salt and freshly ground black pepper, then pour the dressing over the top. Toss to coat well and serve.

FOREST BEAN SALAD
WITH HERB LEMON DRESSING

Three beans and asparagus make for a wonderful vibrant green salad. With the herb lemon dressing it is a joy to have al fresco on a summer's day, when the vegetables are fresh and at their finest. If you are using fresh broad beans, rather than frozen, add them at the same time as the green beans.

SERVES 4–6

300g (10½oz)
    asparagus spears
150g (5oz) fresh or
    frozen broad beans
250g (9oz) green
    beans, halved
200g (7oz) runner beans,
    sliced on the diagonal
30g (1oz) pumpkin
    seeds, toasted
1 tbsp chia seeds

HERB LEMON
DRESSING

Small bunch of mint,
    leaves chopped
Small bunch of basil,
    leaves chopped
1 large garlic clove, crushed
5 tbsp olive oil
½ green or red chilli,
    deseeded and chopped
Juice of 1 large lemon
2 tsp white wine vinegar
A dash of sugar
A pinch of salt

Mary's Tips

* *Can be assembled 4 hours
    ahead. Dress to serve.*
* *Not suitable for freezing.*

To make the dressing, measure all the ingredients into a small food processor. Whiz until finely chopped and a pesto-like consistency.

Remove the woody ends from the asparagus, then cut the tips from the spears and the stems into rings.

Bring a saucepan of salted water to the boil. Add the broad beans and bring back to the boil. Add the asparagus and the French and runner beans and bring back to the boil again. Boil for 2–3 minutes, until just tender. Drain and refresh in cold water. Drain again and dry on kitchen paper. Place in a large bowl.

Pour the dressing into the bowl and season well with salt and freshly ground black pepper. Toss together and spoon into a serving bowl.

Sprinkle with the pumpkin and chia seeds to serve.

BROCCOLI AND QUINOA SALAD WITH FETA AND YOGHURT DRESSING

This salad is vibrant and hearty; there is only a small amount of quinoa as a base and you could use couscous, if you prefer. The mixed quinoa with red, white and black colours comes in a packet and looks more interesting.

SERVES 4–6

75g (3oz) mixed
    tri-colour quinoa

400g (14oz) tenderstem
    broccoli, trimmed

75g (3oz) pumpkin seeds

2 tbsp olive oil

1 tbsp balsamic glaze

Zest of ½ large lemon

2 small Little Gem lettuce
    hearts, quartered

115g (4oz) feta, crumbled

YOGHURT DRESSING

2 tbsp olive oil

150ml (¼ pint) full-fat
    natural yoghurt

Small bunch of mint,
    leaves picked and
    finely chopped

1 small garlic clove,
    crushed

2 tsp Dijon mustard

A dash of sugar

Juice of ½ large lemon

Mary's Tips

* Assemble up to 4 hours
    ahead. Pour over
    the yoghurt dressing
    just before serving.

* Not suitable for freezing.

Cook the quinoa in boiling water according to the packet instructions. Drain and set aside to cool.

Cook the broccoli in a large saucepan of boiling salted water for 3 minutes, until just tender. Drain and refresh under cold water. Drain again and dry on kitchen paper.

Toast the pumpkin seeds in a small frying pan for a minute or so, until they begin to pop and brown. Set aside to cool.

Combine the olive oil and balsamic glaze in a large bowl. Add the quinoa and lemon zest and season with salt and freshly ground black pepper. Mix well.

To make the yoghurt dressing, measure all the ingredients into a small jug or bowl and mix well.

Spoon the quinoa on to a large, flat serving plate. Arrange the broccoli spears and Little Gem wedges on top. Sprinkle with the feta and toasted pumpkin seeds.

Drizzle the dressing over the top of the salad just before serving.

HISPI CABBAGE NOISETTE

Hispi cabbage, also known as pointed cabbage, is my absolute favourite and I could eat this as a meal on its own. It also goes well with steak.

SERVES 6

1 large Hispi cabbage
75g (3oz) butter
Finely grated zest and
   juice of ½ lemon

Mary's Tips

* *Can be boiled up
   to 4 hours ahead.
   Pan-fry to serve.*
* *Not suitable for freezing.*
* *Drain the cabbage wedges
   well before adding to the
   hot butter in the frying
   pan to prevent spitting.*

Remove any outer distressed leaves of the cabbage and discard. Cut the cabbage into 6 equal wedges lengthways through the root.

Bring a large saucepan of salted water to the boil. Add the cabbage wedges and cook for about 3 minutes. Lift out carefully with a slotted spoon and drain well.

Melt half of the butter in a wide frying pan over a high heat. When it is foaming, add the cabbage wedges and fry each wedge for 2–3 minutes on each side, until dark golden in colour. Transfer to a hot serving plate.

Add the lemon zest and juice and the remaining butter to the frying pan, and melt together. Pour over the cabbage wedges, season with salt and freshly ground black pepper and serve hot.

LEEK AND POTATO GRATIN

This is a great dish for vegetarians or to serve as a side dish alongside a roast or sausages. Add hot milk, rather than cold, as this makes for a quicker smooth sauce.

SERVES 4–6

500g (1lb 2oz) potatoes, peeled and cut into 3cm (1¼in) cubes

2 large leeks, trimmed and thickly sliced

30g (1oz) butter, plus extra for greasing

30g (1oz) plain flour

500ml (18fl oz) hot milk

2 tsp Dijon mustard

75g (3oz) Gruyère, grated

75g (3oz) mature Cheddar, grated

Mary's Tips

* Can be assembled up to 8 hours ahead.

* Not suitable for freezing.

Preheat the oven to 200°C/180°C Fan/Gas 6. Grease a 1.75-litre (3-pint) ovenproof dish.

Bring a large saucepan of salted water to the boil. Add the potatoes and boil for 5 minutes. Add the leeks and boil together for 5 minutes. Drain well and refresh under cold water. Drain again.

Meanwhile, melt the butter in a large saucepan. Add the flour and stir over a medium heat for a few seconds. Pour in the hot milk, whisking until smooth and thickened. Season well with salt and freshly ground black pepper. Stir in the mustard and a third of the cheeses and mix well.

Add the leeks and potatoes to the pan and stir to coat in the sauce.

Spoon into the prepared dish and sprinkle with the remaining cheeses. Bake in the preheated oven for 30–35 minutes, until bubbling and lightly golden on top.

GRILLED COURGETTES WITH GINGER CRUNCH

Courgettes can often be forgotten by adding them to a dish and not celebrating them in their own right – this certainly does that! Thin, young courgettes work best, as they have less water in them than the fatter ones.

SERVES 4

400g (14oz) small or baby courgettes, trimmed and sliced in half lengthways or into wedges
2 tbsp olive oil

GINGER CRUNCH

1 tbsp olive oil
1 tsp grated fresh root ginger
30g (1oz) panko breadcrumbs
Finely grated zest of ½ lemon
½–1 red chilli, deseeded and finely chopped (optional)

Mary's Tips

* Best made and served.
* Not suitable for freezing.

Preheat the grill to high.

Place the courgettes on a baking sheet. Brush with olive oil and season well with salt and freshly ground black pepper. Grill for about 10 minutes, turning halfway, until the courgettes are just cooked, golden and tinged brown at the edges.

Meanwhile, heat the oil for the topping in a frying pan over a high heat. Add the ginger and fry for a few seconds. Add the breadcrumbs and lemon and fry for 1–2 minutes, stirring, until crisp and golden.

Place the courgettes on a serving plate and sprinkle with the crumbs. Scatter over the chilli, if using, and serve at once.

GARLIC ROASTED POATOES
WITH ROSEMARY

Crisp and quick to do, these are all cooked in one large roasting tin.

SERVES 4–6

1kg (2¼lb) small
   new potatoes

3 tbsp olive oil

1 large bulb garlic,
   halved horizontally

3 sprigs of rosemary,
   leaves picked and
   finely chopped

Mary's Tips

* *Best cooked and
   served immediately.*

Preheat the oven to 220°C/200°C Fan/Gas 7.

Cut each potato into 3 slices and place in a roasting tin with the olive oil and garlic bulb halves. Season well with salt and freshly ground black pepper and toss together. Roast in the oven for 30–35 minutes, turning halfway through, until golden and crisp.

Remove from the oven, add the rosemary and toss again.

Sprinkle with sea salt and serve straight away.

HARISSA ROASTED CHANTENAY CARROTS

Chantenay carrots are usually sold without their tops in packs of small, fairly evenly sized, short carrots.

SERVES 4–6

1kg (2¼lb) Chantenay carrots, green tips trimmed and halved lengthways if large

2 tbsp olive oil

1–2 tbsp harissa paste, to taste

Juice of ½ lemon

1 tbsp runny honey

½ bunch of flat-leaf parsley, finely chopped

Mary's Tips

* *Best made and served.*

* *Not suitable for freezing.*

* *Be sure to scrape out the delicious sticky glaze from the base of the roasting tin and serve with the carrots.*

Preheat the oven to 200°C/180°C Fan/Gas 6.

Place the carrots in a roasting tin. Drizzle with the olive oil and season with salt and freshly ground black pepper. Toss together to coat, then spread them out in an even layer. Roast in the oven for about 30 minutes, until the carrots are just cooked and lightly golden brown.

Meanwhile, mix the harissa, lemon juice and honey together in a small bowl.

Spoon the harissa mixture over the carrots and mix well to coat. Return the tin to the oven for another 5–10 minutes, or until the largest carrots are cooked through.

Sprinkle with chopped parsley to serve.

ROASTED MEDITERRANEAN VEGETABLES WITH GOAT'S CHEESE

These roasted veg are a great side dish or you could double up quantities to serve them as a main meal. There's no need to remove the skin from the goat's cheese.

SERVES 6

4 tbsp olive oil

2 small aubergines, sliced into thick half-moons

1 large pepper, deseeded and cut into chunks

1 red onion, sliced into wedges

3 garlic cloves, skin on

3 sprigs of thyme

1 courgette or 200g (7oz) baby courgettes, thickly sliced

115g (4oz) hard goat's cheese, cut into 1.5cm (⅔in) cubes

1 tbsp balsamic glaze

Mary's Tips

* *The veg can be roasted up to 6 hours ahead. Add the goat's cheese and reheat in a hot oven to serve.*

* *Not suitable for freezing.*

Preheat the oven to 220°C/200°C Fan/Gas 7.

Measure 3 tablespoons of the oil into a large roasting tin and preheat in the oven for a few minutes to get hot.

Remove the tin from the oven and add the aubergines, pepper and onion and toss carefully in the hot oil. Scatter over the garlic cloves and thyme sprigs and season well with salt and freshly ground black pepper. Roast in the oven for 15–20 minutes.

Add the courgettes and roast for another 12–15 minutes, or until all the vegetables are tender and golden.

Snip off the end of the garlic cloves and squeeze out the soft garlic from their skins. Mix into the veg.

Add the cubes of goat's cheese and discard the thyme sprigs. Check the seasoning and toss everything together. Drizzle with the remaining oil and the balsamic glaze to serve.

BAKING

THE ULTIMATE
CHOCOLATE BROWNIES

This is our favourite brownie; it has a wrinkled top and a gooey middle.
Perfect for eating as it is or you could add a topping of your choice.

MAKES 24 SQUARES

360g (12½oz) dark chocolate (2 × 180g packets), broken into pieces

225g (8oz) butter, cubed, plus extra for greasing

225g (8oz) light muscovado sugar

4 eggs, beaten

75g (3oz) self-raising flour

1 tsp vanilla extract

75g (3oz) chocolate chips

Mary's Tips

* Can be made up to 2 days ahead.
* Freezes well cooked.

Preheat the oven to 180°C/160°C Fan/Gas 4. Grease and line a 30 × 23cm (12 × 9in) traybake tin with non-stick baking paper.

Place the chocolate and butter in a large heatproof bowl. Place the bowl over a pan of simmering water until melted. Stir to combine.

Remove from the heat and add the sugar and eggs. Mix well until smooth, then add the flour and vanilla and mix again. Stir in the chocolate chips.

Pour the chocolate mixture into the prepared tin and bake for about 45 minutes, until well risen and set around the edges, with a slightly soft centre.

Leave to cool in the tin, then slice into 24 squares.

WHITE CHOCOLATE AND PISTACHIO BLONDIES

A blondie has a close, dense texture very similar to a traditional brownie. It is imperative not to overheat the butter and chocolate, otherwise it will become thick and hard.

MAKES 24 SQUARES

350g (12oz) white
  chocolate, broken
  into pieces
225g (8oz) butter, cubed,
  plus extra for greasing
300g (10½oz) caster sugar
4 eggs, beaten
1 tsp vanilla extract
225g (8oz) plain flour
115g (4oz) pistachios,
  finely chopped

Mary's Tips

* *Can be made up to
  a day ahead.*
* *Freezes well.*

Preheat the oven to 180°C/160°C Fan/Gas 4. Grease and line a 30 × 23cm (12 × 9in) traybake tin with non-stick baking paper.

Place the chocolate and butter in a large heatproof bowl. Place the bowl over a pan of simmering water until melted, making sure you do not overheat. Stir to combine.

Remove from the heat and add the sugar, eggs and vanilla extract. Mix well, then fold in the flour and most of the nuts.

Pour the mixture into the tin and level the top. Sprinkle with the remaining nuts and bake in the preheated oven for 40–45 minutes, until well risen and lightly golden.

Leave to cool in the tin, then slice into 24 squares (see photo on page 222–3).

SALTED CARAMEL BROWNIES

I have never been too keen on salted caramel, but I am beginning to like it! I know it is loved by many, hence using it for a couple of recipes.

MAKES 24 SQUARES

360g (12½oz) dark
  chocolate, broken
  into pieces
225g (8oz) butter, cubed,
  plus extra for greasing
225g (8oz) light
  muscovado sugar
4 eggs, beaten
75g (3oz) self-raising flour
1 tsp vanilla extract
200g (7oz) salted caramel
  sauce from a jar
A pinch of Maldon sea salt
75g (3oz) Biscoff biscuits,
  each broken into 3 pieces

Mary's Tips

* *Can be made up to
  2 days ahead.*
* *Freezes well cooked.*

Preheat the oven to 180°C/160°C Fan/Gas 4. Grease and line a 30 × 23cm (12 × 9in) traybake tin with non-stick baking paper.

Place the chocolate and butter in a large heatproof bowl. Place the bowl over a pan of simmering water until melted. Stir to combine.

Remove from the heat and add the sugar and eggs. Mix well until smooth, then add the flour and vanilla, and mix again.

Place the caramel sauce and sea salt into a small bowl. Mix well.

Pour the chocolate mixture into the base of the prepared tin. Drizzle the salted caramel sauce over the top in a swirly pattern, then scatter with the biscuits and press them down slightly. Bake in the preheated oven for about 45 minutes, or until well risen and set around the edges, with a slightly soft centre.

Leave to cool in the tin, then slice into 24 squares (see photo on page 222–3).

GINGER AND ORANGE POLENTA CAKE

*I adore ginger, and ginger and orange are a winning combination. Polenta
is a traditional Italian cooked cornmeal and can be a combination of grains.
It is used in many dishes, including desserts and porridge, but I like it in a
cake, as it gives a moist, grainy texture to an unusual but special cake.*

SERVES 8

250g (9oz) butter,
  softened, plus extra
  for greasing

250g (9oz) caster sugar

4 eggs, beaten

250g (9oz) ground
  almonds

175g (6oz) polenta

1 tsp baking powder

1½ tbsp ground ginger

Finely grated zest and
  juice of 1 large orange

4 tbsp ginger syrup (from
  the stem ginger jar)

115g (4oz) icing
  sugar, sifted

2–3 stem ginger bulbs,
  finely chopped

Mary's Tips

* *Can be made up to
  a day ahead.*

* *Freezes well un-iced.*

Preheat the oven to 160°C/140°C Fan/Gas 3. Grease
and base-line a 23cm (9in) springform tin with
non-stick baking paper.

Measure the butter and caster sugar into a bowl.
Whisk with an electric hand whisk until pale and
creamy. Add the eggs, a little at a time, whisking
until well incorporated. (The mixture might curdle
a little at this point – don't worry!) Gently fold in the
almonds, polenta, baking powder, ground ginger and
orange zest.

Spoon into the prepared tin and level the top. Bake
in the preheated oven for about 1¼ hours, until pale
golden and coming away from the sides of the tin.

Pour the orange juice over the warm cake and leave
to cool in the tin on a wire rack.

Meanwhile, to make the icing, mix the ginger syrup
and sifted icing sugar together in a small bowl until
a smooth and thickish. Place the cooled cake on to a
plate and spread the icing over the top using a palette
knife. Scatter over the ginger pieces and leave to set
for about 1 hour.

Cut into 8 generous wedges.

HONEYCOMB ROCKY ROAD

A non-bake fridge cake, rocky road goes back a long way. This is great with a cup of coffee or after a meal instead of a pudding.

MAKES 24 SQUARES

400g (14oz) milk chocolate, broken into pieces

225g (8oz) butter, cubed, plus extra for greasing

6 tbsp golden syrup

75g (3oz) dark chocolate, broken into pieces

500g (1lb 2oz) digestive biscuits, roughly crushed to nut-sized pieces

4 × 32g chocolate honeycomb bars, sliced into bite-sized pieces

Mary's Tips

* *Can be made up to 3 days ahead.*

* *Freeze well.*

Grease and line a 30 × 23cm (12 × 9in) traybake tin with non-stick baking paper.

Place the milk chocolate in a large heatproof bowl and add the butter and syrup. Place the bowl over a pan of simmering water and heat gently, stirring, until melted.

Place the dark chocolate into a small heatproof bowl. Place the bowl over a pan of simmering water until melted.

Add the biscuits to the milk chocolate mixture and fold together until well coated. Spoon into the prepared tin. Sprinkle over the chocolate honeycomb pieces and press down firmly. Drizzle with the melted dark chocolate in a zig zag pattern. Chill in the fridge for 2 hours until firm.

Slice into 24 squares.

LEMON AND PASSION FRUIT TRAYBAKE

Traybakes are so versatile and are perfect for sharing or wrapping as gifts. Passion fruit curd is readily available and it is wonderful to be able to buy it so easily as we love it! This recipe also works well with lemon or orange curd instead of passion fruit.

MAKES 16 PIECES

225g (8oz) baking spread, from the fridge, plus extra for greasing

225g (8oz) caster sugar

275g (10oz) self-raising flour

1 level tsp baking powder

4 eggs

2 tbsp milk

2 tbsp passion fruit curd

Finely grated zest of 2 lemons

PASSION ICING

300ml (½ pint) pouring double cream

4 tbsp passion fruit curd

Mary's Tips

* Can be made up to a day ahead. Keep covered in the fridge. Eat within 3 days.

* Freezes well un-iced for up to 1 month.

* If you overwhip the cream and it starts to curdle, save it by adding a little more liquid cream, a spoonful at a time, until it becomes smooth again.

Preheat the oven to 180°C/160°C Fan/Gas 4. Grease and line a 30 × 23 cm (12 × 9in) traybake tin with non-stick baking paper.

Measure all the traybake ingredients into a large bowl and beat with an electric hand whisk until combined and smooth.

Spoon into the prepared tin and level the top. Bake in the preheated oven for about 35 minutes, or until the cake has shrunk from the sides of the tin and springs back when pressed in the centre. Leave to cool in the tin.

To make the passion icing, whip the cream to soft peaks, then fold half the curd into the cream and carefully mix together. (Be careful not to overwhip the cream, as adding the curd will make it thicken further.) Spread the icing over the surface of the cooled cake.

Drizzle the top with the remaining curd in a zig-zag pattern. Cut into 16 pieces.

SALTED CARAMEL CAKE

The light muscovado sugar gives a lovely caramel flavour to the
sponge and the caramel gives a moist texture and moreish cake.

SERVES 8

225g (8oz) baking spread,
  from the fridge
175g (6oz) caster sugar
55g (2oz) light
  muscovado sugar
4 eggs
1 tsp vanilla extract
225g (8oz) self-
  raising flour
1 tsp baking powder
1 tbsp milk
1 × 397g tin Carnation
  caramel
½ tsp fine sea salt

ICING

250g (9oz) butter, very soft
250g (9oz) icing sugar
½ tsp fine sea salt
115g (4oz) salted caramel
  fudge, chopped
  into small pieces

Mary's Tips

* *Can be made up to*
  a day ahead.
* *Freezes well un-iced.*

Preheat the oven to 180°C/160°C Fan/Gas 4. Grease and base-line 2 × 20cm (8in) sandwich tins with non-stick baking paper.

Measure the baking spread, caster and light muscovado sugars, eggs, vanilla, flour, baking powder, milk, 3 tablespoons of the caramel and the salt into a large bowl. Whisk together for 2 minutes using an electric hand whisk.

Spoon into the prepared tins and level the surfaces. Bake in the preheated oven for 25–30 minutes, until well risen and coming away from the sides of the tins. Leave to cool on a wire rack.

Meanwhile, to make the icing, measure the butter and icing sugar into a large bowl. Whisk together with an electric hand whisk until pale and creamy. Add the salt and the remaining caramel from the tin and whisk until just mixed. Make sure you do not overbeat, as it could spilt.

Place one cake on a cake stand and spread a third of the icing over the top. Place the second cake on top. Spread the remaining icing over the sides and top of the cake. Sprinkle with the chopped fudge.

Cut into wedges to serve.

GIN AND LIME DRIZZLE TRAYBAKE

This is fun and will be great for a girls' tea! Men will love it, too, of course, but it's the girls in my life who enjoy a G&T!

MAKES 16 PIECES

225g (8oz) baking spread, from the fridge
225g (8oz) caster sugar
275g (10oz) self-raising flour
1 tsp baking powder
4 eggs
2 tbsp milk
Zest of 2 limes

TOPPING

175g (6oz) granulated sugar
6 tbsp gin
Juice of 2 limes

Mary's Tips

* Can be made up to a day ahead.
* Freezes well

Preheat the oven to 180°C/160°C Fan/Gas 4. Grease and line a 30 × 23 cm (12 × 9in) traybake tin with non-stick baking paper.

Measure all the traybake ingredients into a large bowl and beat with an electric hand whisk until light and fluffy.

Spoon into the prepared tin and level the surface. Bake in the preheated oven for 30–35 minutes, until well risen and lightly golden in colour.

Meanwhile, to make the topping, measure the sugar, gin and lime juice into a bowl and mix well.

When the cake comes out of the oven, pour the sugar mixture over the top of the warm cake and spread out to the edges. Leave to cool in the tin.

Cut into 16 pieces.

CLEMENTINE CAKE

A wonderful and impressive four-layered cake bursting with flavour.

SERVES 6–8

DECORATION

2 clementines

4 tbsp thin-cut orange marmalade

115g (4oz) granulated sugar

CAKE

1 large clementine

225g (8oz) butter, softened

275g (10oz) self-raising flour

275g (10oz) caster sugar

4 eggs

1 tsp baking powder

1 tsp ground mixed spice

1 tsp ground cinnamon

ICING

225g (8oz) butter, softened

350g (12oz) icing sugar, plus extra for dusting

Mary's Tips

* Can be made up to 8 hours ahead.
* Freezes well un-iced.

Make the decoration ahead so it has time to crystallise. Line a large baking sheet with non-stick baking paper. Peel two clementines, keeping the peel in a large piece. Roll up the peel and slice thinly to make long, very thin strips.

Measure the marmalade into a small saucepan and add 2 tablespoons of water. Place over a low heat, stirring until the marmalade has dissolved. Add the strips of peel and simmer gently for 5 minutes, stirring until the peel is sticky.

Meanwhile, sprinkle the granulated sugar on to a large dinner plate. Add the sticky peel and toss in the sugar. Spoon on to the prepared tray, separating any strips that have stuck together, and leave to dry out for a few hours.

Preheat the oven to 180°C/160°C Fan/Gas 4. Grease and base-line 2 × 20cm (8in) sandwich tins with non-stick baking paper.

To make the cake, place the large clementine, whole and unpeeled, into a saucepan. Cover with water and a lid. Bring up to the boil, then reduce the heat and simmer for about 20 minutes, or until the clementine is soft and tender. Drain and leave to cool.

Slice the cooled clementine in half and remove any pips. Cut each half in half again and place in a food processor. Whiz until a chunky consistency.

recipe continues overleaf...

Measure all the remaining cake ingredients into a large bowl. Whisk for 2 minutes with an electric hand whisk, until light and fluffy.

Stir half of the clementine pulp into the batter (reserving the rest for the icing).

Divide the cake mixture between the two prepared tins and level the top. Bake in the preheated oven for 25–30 minutes, until well risen and pale golden. Leave to cool on a wire rack for about 10 minutes, then turn out and peel off the baking paper. Leave to cool completely.

Meanwhile, to make the icing, measure the butter and half of the icing sugar into a bowl. Add the remaining clementine pulp and whisk together, using an electric hand whisk, until well combined. Add the remaining icing sugar and whisk again until light and fluffy.

Place each cake on a board and, using a bread knife, carefully and slowly slice each one in half horizontally to give four thin cakes. Sit one on a plate and spread a quarter of the icing carefully over the top, right to the edge. Continue stacking the cakes and spreading with icing until you have four layers of cake and icing.

Swirl the icing on the top cake and arrange the crystallised clementine in a ring on top. Dust with icing sugar to serve.

BIRTHDAY CHOCOLATE GANACHE CAKE

An all-in-one chocolate cake with a deliciously naughty icing, too!

SERVES 8–10

CAKE

55g (2oz) cocoa powder

6 tbsp boiling water

4 eggs

175g (6oz) self-raising flour

1 level tsp baking powder

115g (4oz) baking spread from the fridge, plus extra for greasing

250g (9oz) caster sugar

GANACHE ICING

300ml (½ pint) pouring double cream

300g (10½oz) dark chocolate, broken into pieces

DECORATION

3 tbsp apricot jam, warmed

6 white chocolate Lindt balls

3 large strawberries, halved, keeping the green stem attached

30g (1oz) dark chocolate, melted

Preheat the oven to 180°C/160°C Fan/Gas 4. Grease and base line 2 × 20cm (8in) sandwich tins with non-stick baking paper.

To make the cake, measure the cocoa and boiling water into a large bowl. Mix well to make a smooth paste.

Add the remaining cake ingredients and whisk, using an electric hand whisk, until light and smooth with an even chocolate colour.

Divide the cake mixture between the prepared tins and level the surface. Bake in the preheated oven for 25–30 minutes, or until well risen, shrinking away from the sides of the tin and springy to the touch.

Leave for 10 minutes to cool in the tins, then carefully place on a wire rack and allow to cool completely.

To make the ganache icing, pour the cream into a small saucepan and heat until piping hot, but don't allow it to boil. Remove from the heat, add the chocolate pieces and stir until smooth and shiny.

Set aside in a cool place (but not the fridge) and leave to thicken to a spreadable consistency. Divide the icing into three.

Spread the tops of each cooled cake with apricot jam. Spread one of the cakes with a third of the icing, then place the other cake on top.

recipe continues overleaf...

* Best made and
  assembled on the day
  up to 6 hours ahead.

* Freezes well un-iced.

Spread another third of the icing on the top, then use a small palette knife to make a pretty swirl pattern.

Spoon the final third of icing into a piping bag fitted with a rose nozzle. Pipe large rosettes on one section of the cake. Pile the white chocolate balls on top of the rosettes, placing them so that they gradually cascade on to the top of the cake.

Decorate the surface of the cake with the halved strawberries, then use a teaspoon or small piping bag to drizzle the melted dark chocolate in a zig-zag pattern over the white balls and the top of the cake.

Add candles for a Happy Birthday!

SHIRL'S FRUIT CAKE

*My dear friend Shirl gave me this cake for tea one day and, oh, it was
so good. She has been making it for years. Simmering the sultanas makes
the fruit plump much more quickly than soaking them overnight.*

SERVES 8-10

450g (1lb) sultanas
150ml (¼ pint) orange
   juice, from a carton
225g (8oz) butter, softened
3 eggs, beaten
175g (6oz) caster sugar
225g (8oz) self-
   raising flour

Mary's Tips

* *Can be made up to
   3 days ahead.*
* *Freezes well.*

Preheat the oven to 180°C/160°C Fan/Gas 4. Line
the base and sides of a 20cm (8in) deep cake tin with
non-stick baking paper.

Place the sultanas in a saucepan. Cover with the
orange juice and bring up to the boil. Reduce the
heat and simmer for about 2 minutes to plump up
the sultanas. Drain them, if necessary, and set aside.

Place the butter in a large bowl. Add the warm
sultanas and stir until the butter has melted. Add all
the remaining ingredients and beat well.

Spoon into the tin and level the top. Bake in the
preheated oven for 1 hour–1 hour 20 minutes, until
lightly golden brown. (If the cake is browning too
quickly, cover the top with foil.) Insert a skewer into
the centre of the cake; if it comes out clean then the
cake is cooked. Cool in the tin on a wire rack.

Cut into wedges to serve.

STAR ALMOND MINCE PIES

Using marzipan as a lid, instead of pastry, makes a delicious change. Use white or golden marzipan; we prefer golden for this recipe. The almond pastry is just as easy to make as classic shortcrust. This recipe is perfect for cooking with children. Making these is a joy and sharing the love of food is always a pleasure. If you don't have a star cutter, cut the stars by hand; it's great fun to do!

MAKES 24

1 × 410g jar luxury
  mincemeat
Zest of 1 orange
Icing sugar, for dusting
250g (9oz) marzipan
1 egg, beaten

PASTRY

150g (5oz) plain flour,
  plus extra for dusting
30g (1oz) ground almonds
115g (4oz) butter
30g (1oz) caster sugar
1 egg, beaten

Mary's Tips

* *The pastry can be
  prepared ahead and kept
  in the fridge for 1–2 days
  or frozen. The mince
  pies can be made up to
  2 days ahead. Store in
  an airtight container.*

* *Freeze well cooked.*

You will need 2 × 12-hole bun tins, a 7cm (2¾in) flute cutter and a 5cm (2in) star cutter.

First make the pastry. Measure the flour, ground almonds, butter and caster sugar into a food processor. Whiz until breadcrumb stage. Add the egg and whiz again until a ball is formed. Bring the pastry together and place on a floured work surface. Roll out thinly, then use the fluted cutter to stamp out 24 rounds. Line the bun tins and prick the bases with a fork. Chill in the fridge for at least 30 minutes.

Preheat the oven to 200°C/180°C Fan/Gas 6.

Spoon the mincemeat into a bowl. Add the orange zest and mix to combine. Spoon about 1 teaspoon of the mincemeat into each pastry case.

Dust the work surface with a little icing sugar and roll out the marzipan to roughly 2–3mm (¹⁄₁₆–⅛in) thick. Stamp out star shapes with the star cutter and place them on top of the mincemeat.

Brush the pastry edge and marzipan stars with beaten egg, then bake the pies in the oven for 15–18 minutes, until golden and crisp on top and underneath.

Leave to cool for 5 minutes, then release them from the tins and place on a wire rack.

Serve warm, dusted with icing sugar and brandy cream on the side, if you want to spoil yourself!

BANANA FRUIT BREAD

A little different to everyone's banana bread, the addition of the sultanas and apricots gives it extra interest and moisture.

MAKES A 900G (2LB) LOAF

115g (4oz) butter, softened, plus extra for greasing

75g (3oz) light muscovado sugar

75g (3oz) caster sugar

200g (7oz) over-ripe bananas, mashed (peeled weight)

2 eggs

225g (8oz) self-raising flour

1 tsp baking powder

2 tbsp milk

55g (2oz) sultanas

30g (1oz) dried apricots, chopped

Icing sugar, for dusting

Mary's Tips

* Can be made and kept for 2 days.

* Freezes well.

* Buy recyclable paper loaf tin liners for a quick way to line the tins. These are perfect to transport the cakes to friends or for cake sales.

Preheat the oven to 160°C/140°C Fan/Gas 3. Grease and line a 900g (2lb) loaf tin with non-stick baking paper.

Measure all the ingredients, except the sultanas, apricots and icing sugar, into a large bowl. Whisk together using an electric hand whisk until light and fluffy. Stir in the sultanas and apricots, making sure they are evenly distributed.

Spoon into the tin and level the surface. Bake in the preheated oven for 1 hour–1 hour 20 minutes until lightly golden, well risen and firm to the touch. (If the loaf browns too quickly, cover the top with foil.)

Allow to cool in the tin for 10 minutes, then lift out on to a wire rack and remove the paper. Leave to cool completely.

Dust the loaf with icing sugar and serve in slices with butter.

EASTER SIMNEL CAKE

This has become the traditional Easter cake, but originally it was given by servant girls to their mothers when they went home on Mothering Sunday. The cake would have been made by the servant girl with the help of the cook in charge. I think this is my all-time favourite cake, along with a good Madeira cake. Don't expect the marzipan in the centre to remain as a golden layer; when baked it will darken and sink a little but it tastes wonderful!

SERVES 8–10

175g (6oz) light muscovado sugar

175g (6oz) butter, softened, plus extra for greasing

175g (6oz) self-raising flour

3 eggs

30g (1oz) ground almonds

2 tbsp milk

1 tsp ground mixed spice

2 tsp ground ginger

115g (4oz) sultanas

115g (4oz) glacé cherries, quartered, washed and dried

115g (4oz) dried apricots, snipped into small pieces

115g (4oz) stem ginger bulbs, finely chopped

DECORATION

Icing sugar, for dusting

450g (1lb) golden marzipan

3 tbsp apricot jam, warmed

1 egg, beaten

Crystallised flowers, to decorate

Preheat the oven to 150°C/130°C Fan/Gas 2. Grease and line a 20cm (8in) round, deep cake tin with non-stick baking paper.

Measure all the cake ingredients, except the dried fruit and stem ginger, into a large bowl and beat well with an electric hand whisk until thoroughly blended. Stir in the fruit and stem ginger.

Spoon half the mixture into the prepared tin and level the surface.

Dust the work surface with a little icing sugar, then take one third of the marzipan and roll it into a circle the same size as the cake tin. Place the circle of marzipan on top of the cake mixture in the tin, then spoon the remaining cake mixture on top. Level the surface. Bake in the preheated oven for 1¾–2 hours, or until golden brown and firm in the middle. (If towards the end of the cooking time, the cake is getting too brown, cover the top loosely with foil.) Once baked, the cake is not very deep. Allow the cake to cool in the tin before turning on to a wire rack.

Brush the top of the cooled cake with a little apricot jam. Roll out half the remaining marzipan to the size of the cake and sit it on the top of the cake. Crimp the edges of the marzipan with your finger and thumb and, using a sharp knife, make a lattice pattern in the centre. Use the remaining marzipan to make 11 even-sized balls and arrange them around the edge, fixing them in place with a little beaten egg.

Preheat the grill to high, if using.

Brush the decorated cake with the beaten egg, then place under the grill for about 5 minutes to glaze, turning the cake around so it browns evenly, until the marzipan is tinged brown all over. (This can also be done with a blowtorch, if preferred.)

Decorate with crystallised flowers (see photo on page 250–1).

To crystallise primroses or violets, arrange the fresh flowers on a wire rack. Lightly whisk an egg white in a bowl, then carefully brush over the flower petals. Sprinkle caster sugar over the flowers so the sugar sticks to the egg white and covers the petals evenly. Leave them to harden in a warm place, e.g. a shelf above a radiator or in an airing cupboard, until dry and firm.

POSH WHITE CHOCOLATE SHORTBREAD BISCUITS

So moreish and great to gift wrap in a box. Add a ribbon and label and share with a friend or neighbour – homemade treats are simply the best to bring a smile.

MAKES 25

175g (6oz) plain flour, plus extra for dusting

175g (6oz) butter at room temperature, cubed

75g (3oz) ground almonds

75g (3oz) icing sugar

1 tsp vanilla extract

180g (6½oz) white chocolate, broken into pieces

Mary's Tips

* Can be made up to a day ahead.

* Freeze well undipped. Defrost, refresh in moderate oven, then cool and dip.

Preheat the oven to 180°C/160°C Fan/Gas 4. You will need two baking sheets lined with non-tick baking paper and a 6cm (2½in) round cutter.

Measure the flour, butter, almonds, icing sugar and vanilla extract into a food processor. Whiz until the mixture comes together into a smooth dough.

Lightly dust a work surface with flour. Remove the dough from the bowl and shape into a ball. Using a floured rolling pin, roll out to about 3mm (⅛in) thick. Stamp out rounds using the round cutter and place on the baking sheets, arranging them so there is space between each one. Bake for 15–18 minutes until pale golden. Carefully remove from the trays with a fish slice and leave to cool on a wire rack.

Place the white chocolate in a small heatproof bowl over a pan of simmering water until melted.

Spoon the chocolate over the biscuits in a zig-zag pattern or, if preferred, you could dip half of each biscuit into the melted chocolate to coat one side. Leave to set on a wire rack until hard.

TEAR AND SHARE
CHEESE AND HERB ROLLS

So impressive to make and perfect for sharing.

MAKES 32

500g (1lb 2oz) strong
   bread flour, plus
   extra for dusting

1 × 7g packet of dried
   fast-action yeast

1½ tsp salt

1 tbsp olive oil

350ml (12fl oz)
   warm water

115g (4oz) mature
   Cheddar, grated

4 tbsp chopped fresh
   herbs (e.g. rosemary,
   thyme, chives, basil)

1 egg, beaten

Mary's Tips

* *Best made and
   served on the day.*

* *Freezes well cooked.
   Defrost and refresh in a
   moderate oven to serve.*

Measure the flour, yeast, salt, olive oil and water into a free-standing mixer. Mix well using the dough hook until the dough comes together. You may need to add a little more water, if it looks dry.

Tip the dough on to a floured work surface and knead for about 5 minutes, until it is soft and smooth. Place in an oiled bowl, cover tightly with cling film and leave to rise in a warm place for 2 hours, or until doubled in size.

Preheat the oven to 220°C/200°C Fan/Gas 7. Line a baking sheet with non-stick baking paper.

Tip the dough on to a floured work surface and knead (or 'knock back') for 2–3 minutes. Flatten out the dough to a round about 20cm (8in) diameter, add the cheese and herbs, then firmly knead the ingredients into the dough until well distributed. Shape into 32 even-sized balls.

Arrange the balls on the prepared baking sheet in a round shape, so they are slightly touching. Cover with a clean tea towel and leave to prove in a warm place for 30 minutes, or until well risen and almost doubled in size.

Brush the surface of the rolls with the beaten egg and bake in the preheated oven for 25–30 minutes, until well risen and golden brown on top and underneath. Slide on to a wire rack to cool slightly.

Serve warm.

PUDDINGS
AND DESSERTS

TIRAMISU RED FRUIT TRIFLE

*The addition of red fruits turns this tiramisu into a trifle bursting
with fruit flavours. I like to use brandy for soaking the sponges,
but you could use rum, kirsch or Baileys if you prefer.*

SERVES 10–12

500g (1lb 2oz) frozen red
  fruits e.g. raspberries,
  blackberries and cherries

55g (2oz) caster sugar

1 heaped tbsp cornflour

250g (9oz) full-fat
  mascarpone cheese

6 tbsp icing sugar, sifted

1 tbsp vanilla extract

600ml (1 pint) pouring
  double cream

450ml (¾ pint) strong
  coffee, cooled

40ml (1½fl oz) brandy

12 trifle sponges,
  each sliced in half
  horizontally

115g (4oz) dark chocolate,
  coarsely grated

You will need a round shallow glass dish about 8cm
(3¼in) high and 25cm (10in) diameter.

Measure the fruits and caster sugar into a saucepan.
Place over a medium heat, stirring, until the sugar has
dissolved. Transfer the fruits into a sieve over a bowl
(do not press them, as you want to leave them whole).
Pour the liquid from the bowl back into the saucepan.

In a small bowl, mix the cornflour with 2 tablespoons
of water until smooth. Add this to the fruit liquid in
the saucepan and mix. Stir over a medium heat until
thickened. Remove from the heat and add the whole
fruits. Set aside to become cold.

Measure the mascarpone, icing sugar and vanilla into a
large bowl and blend together. Add the cream and whisk
with an electric whisk for a few minutes to soft peaks.

Mix the coffee and brandy together in a shallow dish.

Dip half of the sponge halves in the coffee mixture,
soaking them well. Arrange them tightly over the base
of the glass dish. Spread a third of the cream mixture
on top and sprinkle with half the chocolate. Spoon all
the fruits on top in an even layer. Soak the remaining
sponges in the coffee mixture and use them to cover the
fruits. Spread half the remaining cream over the top
and sprinkle with the remaining chocolate.

Finally, place the remaining cream mixture into a piping
bag fitted with a 1cm (½in) plain nozzle and pipe blobs
around the edge. Chill for 1–2 hours before serving.

HAZELNUT MERINGUE ROULADE WITH BRANDY CREAM

Meringue and hazelnuts are a class combination. Meringue roulade may seem tricky to make, but it is fairly straightforward if you read the recipe carefully!

SERVES 8–10

Butter, for greasing

5 egg whites

275g (10oz) caster sugar

55g (2oz) roasted hazelnuts, roughly chopped

300ml (½ pint) pouring double cream

2 tbsp Baileys cream liqueur or brandy

225g (8oz) raspberries

Mary's Tips

* *Best made on the day.*

* *Freezes well rolled but the surface does not remain crisp.*

Preheat the oven to 200°C/180°C Fan/Gas 6. Line a 33 × 23cm (13 × 9in) Swiss roll tin with greased non-stick baking paper.

Whisk the egg whites in a mixer on full speed or with an electric whisk until very stiff. Gradually add the sugar, a heaped teaspoon at a time, whisking at high speed all the time. Whisk until very, very stiff and glossy and all the sugar has been included.

Carefully fold two-thirds of the hazelnuts into the meringue mixture. Spread into the prepared tin and sprinkle the remaining hazelnuts evenly over the top. Bake in the preheated oven for about 12 minutes or until pale cream in colour.

Lower the oven temperature to 160°C/140°C Fan/Gas 3 and continue to bake for a further 20 minutes until firm to the touch.

Remove the meringue from the oven and leave to cool for a few minutes. Turn it out on to a sheet of non-stick baking paper, hazelnut side down. Remove the paper from the base of the meringue and leave to cool completely.

Whip the cream in a large bowl to soft peaks, then stir in the Baileys or brandy. Fold in the raspberries. Spread the raspberry cream over the meringue to the edges. Starting to roll from a long side, roll the meringue tightly like a Swiss roll. Wrap the rolled meringue in non-stick baking paper and chill in the fridge.

Transfer to a large serving plate and gently remove the baking paper to serve.

GLORIOUS CHOCOLATE TRUFFLE DESSERT

Decadent, indulgent, impressive, delicious — all the fancy words describe this dessert — a real celebration of chocolate. It takes a bit of time, but is so worth making for a special occasion.

SERVES 8–10

CHOCOLATE CAKE

Butter, for greasing
250g (9oz) dark chocolate, broken into pieces
6 eggs, 5 of them separated
225g (8oz) caster sugar
150g (5oz) ground almonds

TRUFFLE FILLING

180g (6½oz) dark chocolate, broken into pieces
75g (3oz) caster sugar
1 tbsp brandy
3 egg yolks, beaten
300ml (½ pint) pouring double cream

DECORATION

Cocoa powder, for dusting
200ml (⅓ pint) pouring double cream
4 chocolate truffles, halved

Preheat the oven to 200°C/180°C Fan/Gas 6. Grease and base line 2 × 20cm (8in) loose-bottomed sandwich or springform tins.

To make the chocolate cake, place the chocolate in a heatproof bowl over a pan of simmering water until melted. Leave to cool a little.

Whisk the 5 egg whites in a large mixing bowl with an electric whisk until stiff but not dry.

In a separate large bowl, use an electric whisk to whisk together the 5 egg yolks, the remaining whole egg and the sugar until thick and light in colour. The mixture should be thick enough to leave a trail when the whisk is lifted from the bowl.

Stir in the almonds, melted chocolate and 1 tablespoon of the whisked egg whites. Carefully fold in the remaining egg whites using a metal spoon. Mix carefully until combined, without knocking any air out of the mixture.

Spoon into the prepared tins and gently tilt the tins to level the surface. Bake in the preheated oven for 25–30 minutes, or until a slight crust forms on the top and the cakes have started to shrink away from the sides of the tins. Leave to cool in the tins for about 10 minutes, then turn out on to a wire rack.

Mary's Tips

* _Can be made up to_
  a day ahead.
* _Freezes well._
  Decorate to serve.

While the cakes are cooling, make the truffle filling. Place the chocolate pieces in a food processor and whiz until finely chopped.

Measure the sugar and 6 tablespoons of water into a small saucepan and stir over a low heat until the sugar has dissolved. Bring up to the boil and boil for 20 seconds. Pour this sugar syrup into the processor while the motor is running to melt the chocolate. Scape down the sides of the bowl to make sure there are no lumps. Add the brandy and egg yolks and whiz again. Spoon into a bowl.

In a separate large bowl, use an electric whisk to whisk the cream to stiff peaks. Fold the cream into the chocolate and brandy mixture.

Grease and line the sides of a deep 20cm (8in) loose-bottomed cake or springform tin with non-stick baking paper. Place one cake into the base of the springform tin top side down and press down firmly. Spoon the mousse filling on top and spread to the edges. Place the second cake top side up on top and press gently. Sprinkle the top with cocoa powder and chill in the fridge for 6 hours.

When ready to serve, remove the tin and transfer to a serving plate. Whip the cream to soft peaks and spoon into a piping bag fitted with a rosette nozzle. Pipe 8 large rosettes on top and place half a chocolate truffle in each one (see photo on pages 264–5).

FEATHERED WHITE CHOCOLATE CHEESECAKE

This is a dessert to impress – feathering the top looks stunning and is easier than it looks! It's important to have the mascarpone at room temperature to ensure it doesn't go lumpy when mixed with the cream filling.

SERVES 6–8

BASE

125g (4½oz) digestive biscuits

60g (2¼oz) butter, melted, plus extra for greasing

1 tsp demerara sugar

FILLING

200g (7oz) white chocolate, broken into pieces

250g (9oz) full-fat mascarpone cheese at room temperature

300ml (½ pint) pouring double cream

1 tsp vanilla extract

DECORATION

115g (4oz) dark chocolate, broken into pieces

100ml (3½fl oz) pouring double cream

30g (1oz) white chocolate

Mary's Tips

* *Can be made up to a day ahead.*

* *Freezes well.*

Grease and base-line a 20cm (8in) sandwich tin with non-stick baking paper.

Place the biscuits in a bag and crush to crumbs with a rolling pin. Tip into a bowl, add the melted butter and demerara sugar and mix well. Spoon into the base of the tin and press down firmly with the back of a spoon. Leave to chill in the fridge for 30 minutes.

Place the white chocolate pieces in a heatproof bowl over a pan of very hot water for a few minutes, until melted. Set aside.

Beat the mascarpone with a little cream to loosen the mixture, then slowly blend in the rest of the cream, stirring until smooth. Add the vanilla and the melted white chocolate. Mix carefully, making sure you don't overbeat. Pour into the tin and level the surface. Chill for 8 hours, or overnight, until set. Remove the base and paper from the cheesecake and slide on to a serving plate.

Place the dark chocolate and cream in a small saucepan and heat gently until the chocolate has melted. Place the white chocolate in a heatproof bowl over a pan of very hot water for a few minutes, until melted. Spoon into a small piping bag.

Pour the plain chocolate and cream mixture over the cheesecake, spreading it out to the edges. Pipe 8 lines of white chocolate across the top. Using a cocktail stick, drag the white lines in alternate directions to make a feathered effect across the top. Chill until set.

CHOCOLATE AND BRANDY SHOTS

The quickest chocolate mousse you will ever make – no gelatine and no raw eggs. It is very rich, but perfect for a few mouthfuls after a meal. Serve in small espresso cups or shot glasses.

SERVES 8–10

200g (7oz) dark chocolate
2 tbsp brandy
150ml (¼ pint) pouring double cream
250g (9oz) full-fat mascarpone cheese at room temperature

Mary's Tips

* Can be made up to 2 days ahead.

* Not suitable for freezing.

You will need 8 or 10 small coffee cups or shot glasses.

Remove 2 squares of chocolate and grate them. Set aside for garnish.

Break the remaining the chocolate into a pan, pour in the brandy and cream, and heat gently until melted, smooth and a uniform chocolate colour throughout. Set aside to cool slightly.

Spoon the mascarpone into a large bowl. Stir well so that it's a smooth paste, then gradually add the melted chocolate mixture and blend until smooth.

Pour into shot glasses or coffee cups. Sprinkle the grated chocolate on top and chill in the fridge for at least 2 hours.

Serve chilled.

LIMONCELLO PASSION PANNA COTTA

Ideal for a dinner party or a buffet table, these are super impressive and light. Leaf gelatine can come in different sizes depending on the brand. We use the platinum grade leaf gelatine, which we have been able to buy in all major supermarkets.

SERVES 6

Sunflower, for greasing

3 sheets of platinum grade leaf gelatine

600ml (1 pint) pouring double cream

55g (2 oz) caster sugar

Finely grated zest of 2 lemons

4 tbsp limoncello

TO SERVE

3 ripe passion fruit, halved

4 tbsp lemon curd

Mary's Tips

* Can be made up to a day ahead. Can turn out up to an hour before serving.

* Not suitable for freezing.

* Scalding point is just too hot to keep your finger in.

Grease the base and sides of six 150ml (¼ pint) metal pudding basins and sit on a baking sheet.

Half fill a small bowl with water. Add the gelatine leaves and leave to become soft for about 5 minutes.

Measure the cream, sugar and lemon zest into a saucepan. Bring to scalding point, stirring, until the sugar has dissolved and the cream is smooth. Add the limoncello. Remove from the heat and cool slightly until hand hot.

Squeeze any water from the gelatine leaves and add the leaves to the warm cream. Whisk until smooth and completely dissolved. Pour the lemon cream mixture into the pudding basins and transfer to the fridge to set for about 6 hours or overnight.

Scoop out the seeds and any juice from the passion fruit and place in a bowl. Stir in the lemon curd. Mix well.

Carefully turn out the panna cotta by running a knife around the edges of the basins and upturning on to a plate. Serve each one with a spoonful of passion lemon curd cascading over the top.

BAKED RICOTTA CHEESECAKE WITH BLACKBERRY COULIS

*Classic vanilla baked cheesecake with a soured cream topping and
a sharp coulis, which complements the creaminess of the cheesecake.
If fresh blackberries are not in season, use frozen instead.*

SERVES 6–8

BASE

125g (4½oz) digestive
   biscuits
75g (3oz) butter, melted,
   plus extra for greasing

FILLING

500g (1lb 2oz) full-
   fat ricotta cheese
180g (6½oz) full-fat
   cream cheese
125g (4½oz) caster sugar
2 eggs
1 tbsp plain flour
1 tsp vanilla extract
Zest of 1 lemon
Juice of ½ lemon
100ml (3½fl oz) pouring
   double cream

TOPPING

800g (1¾lb) blackberries
4 tbsp icing sugar
2 tsp cornflour
200ml (⅓ pint) soured cream

Mary's Tips

* Cheesecake and coulis
   can be made a day ahead.
   Add topping to serve.
* Freezes well without
   the topping.

Preheat the oven to 160°C/140°C Fan/Gas 3. Grease and
base line a 20cm (8in) loose-bottomed or springform tin.

Place the biscuits in a bag and crush to crumbs with
a rolling pin. Tip into a bowl, add the melted butter
and mix well. Spoon into the base of the tin and level
the surface. Press down firmly and chill in the fridge.

Measure the ricotta and cream cheese into a bowl.
Gently whisk until smooth, being careful not to
overwhisk. Add all the remaining filling ingredients
and continue to mix slowly until you have a smooth,
silky consistency, being careful not to overwhisk.

Pour the filling on top of the biscuit base and spread
evenly to the sides. Bake in the preheated oven for
about 1 hour, until slightly golden and just set in the
middle. Turn off the oven and leave to cool inside the
oven for 1 hour until cold. Remove from the tin and
chill in the fridge.

Meanwhile, place the blackberries in a food processor
and whiz until puréed. Pass the purée through a sieve
into a bowl. Add the icing sugar and cornflour to
the bowl, mix well, then tip into a saucepan. Place
over a low heat and stir gently until the mixture has
thickened and coats the back of a spoon. Leave to cool.

Spread the soured cream over the top of the cold
cheesecake. Drizzle a few teaspoons of blackberry
coulis over the top and swirl to make a pretty pattern.
Serve with the remaining coulis alongside.

SPICED APPLE STRUDEL

*Apple strudel used to be such a popular recipe and we think it deserves
a comeback. This would also be delicious with apple and pear, poached
plums or cooked summer fruits. The breadcrumbs help to absorb some
of the liquid from the apples and prevents the pastry from going soggy.
Folding in the ends of the pastry first gives neat ends to the strudel.*

SERVES 6

About 6 sheets of
  filo pastry
About 55g (2oz)
  butter, melted
About 30g (1oz) fresh
  white breadcrumbs

FILLING

2 large cooking apples,
  peeled, cored and sliced
Zest and juice of ½ lemon
55g (2oz) demerara sugar
1 tsp ground mixed spice

ICING

175g (6oz) icing
  sugar, sifted
3–4 tbsp fresh lemon juice

Mary's Tips

* Can be made up to
  a day ahead.
* Freezes well uncooked.

Preheat the oven to 190°C/170°C Fan/Gas 5.

To make the filling, place the apple slices into a bowl
with the lemon zest and juice, and the demerara sugar
and mixed spice. Mix together to combine.

Place 3 sheets of filo side by side (vertically) on a piece
of non-stick baking paper, slightly overlapping the
pastry sheets where they meet. Brush generously with
melted butter. Place 3 sheets of pastry horizontally over
the top, slightly overlapping where they join. Brush
generously with melted butter.

Sprinkle the breadcrumbs over the bottom third of the
pastry about 5cm (2in) away from the edge and sides.
Spoon the apple filling on top of the breadcrumbs.
Fold in the thin ends of the pastry, then fold up the
long edge nearest to you, over the apple filling. Fold
down the remaining long flap of pastry (furthest away
from you) to make an enclosed parcel.

Brush all over with melted butter and transfer the
strudel and the baking paper to a baking sheet. Bake
in the preheated oven for 30–35 minutes until the
pastry is golden and crisp all over.

To make the icing, place the icing sugar in a bowl
and mix in the lemon juice gradually, a little at a time,
to make a thick icing. Drizzle over the strudel in a
random pattern.

Serve warm with cream.

WINDFALL PIE

Crisp shortcrust pastry, tender pink rhubarb and fallen cooking apples –
a simple pie your granny might have made. If you can only get late season
green rhubarb, you may need to add more sugar to the filling.

SERVES 6–8

400g (14oz) young pink
rhubarb, cut into
1cm (½in) pieces

450g (1lb) cooking apples,
peeled, cored and cut
into 2cm (¾in) cubes

115g (4oz) caster sugar

1 tbsp cornflour

A little beaten egg

A sprinkle of
demerara sugar

PASTRY

115g (4oz) butter, cubed

175g (6oz) plain flour,
plus extra for dusting

1 heaped tbsp icing sugar

1 egg, beaten

Mary's Tips

* *Can be assembled up to
8 hours ahead. Reheats
well after cooking.*

* *Freezes well uncooked.*

Preheat the oven to 200°C/180°C Fan/Gas 6. You
will need a 28cm (11in) deep pie dish.

To make the pastry, measure the butter and flour
into a food processor and whiz until breadcrumb
stage. Add the icing sugar and egg and whiz again
until it forms a ball. (You can do this by rubbing in
by hand, if preferred.)

Place the rhubarb, apple, caster sugar and cornflour
into the pie dish. Toss together to mix well. Brush
the edge of the dish with a little beaten egg.

Roll the pastry out to a round slightly bigger than the
surface of the dish. Place over the top of the rhubarb
and apple mixture, and press down and crimp the
edges. Trim the pastry and brush the surface with
beaten egg. Reroll the trimmings and stamp out
rounds using a 4.5cm (1¾in) fluted cutter. Stamp out
the insides using a smaller 2cm (¾in) fluted cutter to
make rings. Arrange the rings in a neat pattern on top
of the pastry. Brush with more egg and sprinkle the
surface with demerara sugar. Bake in the preheated
oven for 30–40 minutes until golden brown. (If the
pie starts to get too brown, cover the top with foil.)

Serve warm with custard.

PEAR AND BLUEBERRY GALETTE

A comforting pudding that is so easy and quick to make. This would work well with tinned apricots or peaches as well. If you want to use fresh pears, peel and poach them until tender first.

SERVES 8

75g (3oz) butter, softened, plus extra for greasing

75g (3oz) caster sugar

115g (4oz) self-raising flour

1 tsp baking powder

2 eggs

1 tsp vanilla extract

2 × 400g tins pear halves in natural juice

150g (5oz) fresh blueberries

2–3 tbsp redcurrant jelly

Mary's Tips

* *Best made and served immediately. If you have some left over it reheats well.*

* *Not suitable for freezing.*

Preheat the oven to 200°C/180°C Fan/Gas 6. Grease a 28cm (11in) fluted loose-bottomed tin.

Measure the butter, sugar, flour, baking powder, eggs and vanilla into a bowl. Beat together until smooth. Spread the mixture to cover the base of the tin.

Drain the pear halves and cut each one lengthways into three long strips. Dry with kitchen paper. Arrange cut-side-down over the surface of the batter. Scatter the blueberries in between the pear strips and bake in the preheated oven for 20–25 minutes, until the sponge is lightly golden brown and well risen.

To glaze, melt the redcurrant jelly in a small saucepan over a low heat. Brush over the hot sponge and the fruit to give a shiny glaze.

Leave until just cool enough to handle, then remove from the tin and cut into wedges. Serve warm with cream or crème fraîche.

SUNDAY LUNCH PLUM CRUMBLE CAKE

Just right for those cosy autumn Sundays with your family. Perfect when plums are in season, though this works well with apples or pears, too.

SERVES 8

300g (10½oz) self-raising flour

1 tsp baking powder

225g (8oz) caster sugar

Zest of 1 small lemon

2 eggs, beaten

150g (5oz) butter, melted, plus extra for greasing

300g (10½oz) ripe plums, cut into small cubes

CRUMBLE TOPPING

40g (1½oz) self-raising flour

20g (¾oz) butter, softened

40g (1½oz) demerara sugar

2 tbsp porridge oats

Mary's Tips

* *Can be made up to a day ahead.*

* *Freezes well.*

Preheat the oven to 180°C/160°C Fan/Gas 4. Line the base of a deep 20cm (8in) springform or loose-bottomed tin with non-stick baking paper and grease the sides well.

To make the cake, measure the flour, baking powder and caster sugar into a mixing bowl. Add the lemon zest, eggs and melted butter and beat with a wooden spoon until combined.

Spread half the mixture into the base of the prepared tin and scatter over the plum cubes. Spoon the remaining mixture on top and spread to give a smooth surface.

To make the crumble topping, combine all the ingredients in a bowl and crumble with your fingertips to give a fine mixture. Sprinkle over the top of the cake. Bake in the preheated oven for 1–1¼ hours, until golden brown and when a skewer is inserted in the centre it comes out clean. Run a palette knife around the edges of the tin to loosen, then remove the cake from the tin and discard the baking paper.

Serve warm with custard.

SUNRISE FRUIT SALAD

Fresh, wonderful colour and ideal for a dessert or breakfast.

SERVES 4–6

1 ripe mango, peeled and
   sliced into thin strips
1 small cantaloupe
   melon, peeled and
   cut into cubes
1 small ripe papaya,
   peeled, deseeded
   and cut into thin
   short matchsticks
3 ripe passion fruit, halved
100ml (3½fl oz) orange
   juice, from a carton
Seeds of 1 pomegranate

Mary's Tips

* Can be assembled up
   to 6 hours ahead.
* Not suitable for freezing.

Place the mango, melon and papaya in a large bowl.

Scoop out the seeds and juice from the passion fruit and stir into the fruits. Pour in the orange juice and place in the fridge to chill.

Scatter with pomegranate seeds before serving chilled.

GLAZED FRENCH PEACH TART

*This dessert is as impressive as it is delicious! The recipe works
just as well with nectarines or apricots. It takes a little time to
do but is so worth it, and is a dish you will be proud of.*

SERVES 8–10

55g (2oz) caster sugar

8 large peaches, halved
and thinly sliced

About 75g (3oz)
apricot jam

PASTRY

175g (6oz) plain flour,
plus extra for dusting

115g (4oz) butter, cubed

3 tbsp icing sugar

1 egg, beaten

CRÈME PATISSIERE

6 egg yolks

115g (4oz) caster sugar

55g (2oz) plain flour

1 tbsp cornflour

500ml (18fl oz)
full-fat milk

1 tsp vanilla extract

100ml (3½fl oz) pouring
double cream,
lightly whipped

You will need a 28cm (11in) fluted loose-bottomed
tart tin.

First make the pastry. Measure the flour, butter
and icing sugar into a food processor. Whiz until
breadcrumb stage. Add the egg and whiz again until
a ball is formed.

Dust a worktop with flour and roll out the pastry as
thinly as possible to a little bigger than the tin. Line
the tin with the pastry up the sides, forming a small
lip around the edge. Prick the base with a fork and
chill in the fridge or freezer for 30 minutes.

Preheat the oven to 200°C/180°C Fan/Gas 6.

Line the pastry case with non-stick baking paper and
fill with baking beans. Bake blind for 15 minutes, then
remove the paper and the beans and bake for another
5–10 minutes, until the pastry is pale golden and crisp.
Set aside to cool and lift out the baking beans and
non-stick baking paper.

Meanwhile, to make the crème pat, place the egg
yolks, sugar, flour and cornflour in a large bowl.
Whisk, using an electric whisk, until the mixture is
thick and pale.

Heat the milk in a saucepan until scalding. Slowly
pour the milk into the bowl and continue whisking
until smooth.

recipe continues overleaf...

* *Can be made up to
  8 hours ahead.*
* *Not suitable for freezing.*
* *When making the crème
  pat, ribbon stage is when
  you lift the beaters and
  there is a trail of mixture
  visible like a ribbon.*
* *Use the leftover egg
  whites to make meringues.*

Pour back into the saucepan, add the vanilla and stir constantly over a medium heat until just boiling and the mixture is at thickish ribbon stage (see Tip).

Spoon into a bowl, cover the surface with non-stick baking paper to stop a skin forming and leave to cool.

When the crème pat is cold, fold in the whipped cream. Set aside and chill until needed.

To poach the peaches, measure 200ml (⅓ pint) water and the caster sugar into a wide-based saucepan. Stir to dissolve the sugar, then bring up to the boil and boil for 2 minutes.

Turn down the heat, add the peach slices and simmer gently for a few minutes, until the peaches are just soft, but not falling apart. Strain the peach slices from the syrup and leave to cool completely.

Place the apricot jam in a small saucepan. Place over a low heat and stir until smooth and runny.

Fill the pastry case with the cold crème pat, spreading to the edges. Arrange the slices of peach overlapping in a neat spiral on top. Brush the peach slices and pastry edges with the apricot glaze and place in the fridge for 30 minutes to set before serving.

Cut into wedges and serve at room temperature.

CONVERSION CHART

WEIGHTS

Metric	Imperial
5g	⅛ oz
10g	¼ oz
15g	½ oz
20g	¾ oz
30g	1 oz
35g	1¼ oz
40g	1½ oz
55g	2 oz
60g	2¼ oz
65g	2½ oz
75g	3 oz
90g	3½ oz
115g	4 oz
125g	4½ oz
150g	5 oz
175g	6 oz
200g	7 oz
225g	8 oz
250g	9 oz
275g	10 oz
300g	10½ oz
325g	11½ oz
350g	12 oz
375g	13 oz
400g	14 oz
425g	15 oz
450g	1 lb
500g	1 lb 2 oz
550g	1¼ lb
600g	1 lb 5 oz
650g	1 lb 7 oz
675g	1½ lb
700g	1 lb 9 oz
750g	1 lb 10 oz
800g	1¾ lb
850g	1 lb 14 oz
900g	2 lb
1.3kg	3 lb
1.8kg	4 lb
2.25kg	5 lb

OVEN TEMPERATURES

°C	Fan °C	°F	Gas Mark
120	100	250	½
140	120	275	1
150	130	300	2
160	140	325	3
180	160	350	4
190	170	375	5
200	180	400	6
220	200	425	7
230	210	450	8
240	220	475	9

VOLUME   MEASUREMENTS

Metric	Imperial
30ml	1 fl oz
50ml	2 fl oz
85ml	3 fl oz
100ml	3½ fl oz
125ml	4 fl oz
150ml	5 fl oz (¼ pint)
175ml	6 fl oz
200ml	7 fl oz (⅓ pint)
225ml	8 fl oz
250ml	9 fl oz
300ml	10 fl oz (½ pint)
350ml	12 fl oz
400ml	14 fl oz
450ml	15 fl oz (¾ pint)
500ml	18 fl oz
600ml	1 pint / 20 fl oz
700ml	1¼ pints
900ml	1½ pints
1 litre	1¾ pints
1.2 litres	2 pints
1.25 litres	2¼ pints
1.5 litres	2½ pints
1.75 litres	3 pints
2 litres	3½ pints
2.25 litres	4 pints
2.5 litres	4½ pints
2.75 litres	5 pints
3.4 litres	6 pints
3.9 litres	7 pints
4.5 litres	8 pints (1 gallon)

Metric	Imperial
5mm	¼ in
1cm	½ in
2cm	¾ in
2.5cm	1 in
3cm	1¼ in
4cm	1½ in
5cm	2 in
7.5cm	3 in
10cm	4 in
12.5cm	5 in
15cm	6 in
18cm	7 in
20cm	8 in
23cm	9 in
25cm	10 in
28cm	11 in
30cm	12 in
33cm	13 in
35cm	14 in

RECIPE FINDER BY STYLE

BRUNCH

American-style Pancakes with Bacon and Maple Syrup (p.47)

Bacon and Egg Breakfast Croustades (p.38)

Cauliflower Potato Cakes with Parmesan Sauce (p.91)

Chicken, Avocado and Mango Lettuce Wraps (p.57)

Cinnamon Crepes (p.49)

Eggy Bread Avocado and Ham Sandwich (p.50)

Frittata with Spinach, Feta and Tomatoes (p.42)

Fruit Kebabs with Lemon Dip (p.58)

Match Day Hot Dogs (p.54)

Shakshuka (p.41)

Smashed Avocado, Asparagus and Fried Egg on Sourdough (p.45)

Toasted Brioche with Avocado, Spinach and Bacon (p.52)

SALADS

Broccoli and Quinoa Salad (p.204)

Coronation Coleslaw (p.194)

Forest Bean Salad (p.200)

Greek Salad with Asparagus (p.196)

Hot-smoked Salmon Rice and Asparagus Salad (p.103)

Noodle Nori Salad (p.199)

Rocket, Parmesan and Bean Salad (p.64)

SOUPS

Autumn Leek and Mushroom Soup (p.31)

Roasted Tomato and Basil Soup (p.34)

Summer Soup – Pea, Potato and Basil (p.28)

Winter Parsnip and Chestnut Soup (p.32)

PASTA AND NOODLES

Black Bean Beef Noodle Stir-fry (p.157)

Chicken Spinach Tomato Lasagne (p.129)

Five Veg Pasta (p.178)

Noodle Nori Salad (p.199)

Spaghetti with Peas and Pesto (p.177)

Vegetable Pad Thai (p.167)

PASTRY

Beef Bourguignon Pie (p.153)

Chicken and Spinach Herb Parcel (p.126)

Jumbo Lentil Rolls (p.91)

Jumbo Sausage Rolls (p.88)

Provence Tomato and Garlic Pistou Tart (p.170–1)

Red Pepper, Cheese and Chive Canapé Tarts (p.19)

Salmon en Croûte with Spinach and Dill (p.98–9)

Shepherd's Puff Pastry Pie (p.138)

STIR-FRIES

Black Bean Beef Noodle Stir-fry (p.157)

Duck Breast with Stir-fry Vegetables and Cashew Sauce (p.134)

Prawn Stir-fry wih Ginger, Coconut and Chilli (p.108)

ROASTS

Loin of Stuffed Pork with Crackling and White Wine Gravy (p.151–2)

Roast Rack of Lamb with Celeriac Purée (p.142)

Sticky Short Beef Ribs and Lemon Coleslaw (p.158–9)

Two Roast Chickens with Scalloped Potatoes (p.118–9)

ONE-POT DISHES

Black Bean Beef Noodle Stir-Fry (p.157)

Celery, Blue Cheese and Sage Risotto (p.168)

Chipchip Cassoulet (p.147)

Double Mustard Chicken (p.124)

Garlic Roasted Potatoes with Rosemary (p.212)

Grilled Courgettes with Ginger Crunch (p.210)

Harissa Roasted Chantenay Carrots (p.215)

Hispi Cabbage Noisette (p.207)

Lamb and Chickpea Spiced Stew (p.141)

Leek and Potato Gratin (p.208)

Majorcan-style One Pot Vegetables (p.188)

Prawn Stir-fry wih Ginger, Coconut and Chilli (p.108)

Roasted Mediterranean Vegetables with Goat's Cheese (p.216)

Roasting Tin Spiced

Chicken (p.114)

Sabzi Vegetable Curry (p.184)

Spicy Pork with Sweet Potato and Black-eyed Beans (p.148)

Sunday Best Minted Lamb (p.145)

Thai Green Curry (p.123)

Tuscan Chicken (p.133)

VEGETARIAN

Avocado, Olive and Tomato Blinis (p.24)

Cauliflower Potato Cakes (p.91)

Celery, Blue Cheese and Sage Risotto (168)

Coriander Roasted Vegetables (p.63)

Curried Squash and Paneer Filo Samosas (p.183)

Five Veg Pasta (p.178)

Frittata with Spinach, Feta and Tomatoes (p.42)

Gardener's Stuffed Squash (p.180)

Garlic Parsley Flatbread (p.85)

Halloumi and Sweet Potato Fries with Chilli Dip (p.86)

Harissa Halloumi and Squash Skewers (p.68)

Jumbo Lentil Rolls (p.91)

Majorcan-style One Pot Vegetables (p.188)

Pea and Feta Blinis (p.24)

Porcini, Wild Mushroom and Watercress Gratin (p.174)

Provence Tomato and Garlic Pistou Tart (p.170–1)

Red Pepper, Cheese and Chive Canapé Tarts (p.19)

Sabzi Vegetaable Curry (p.184)

Shakshuka (p.41)

Smashed Avocado, Asparagus and Fried Egg on Sourdough (p.45)

Spaghetti with Peas and Pesto (p.177)

Vegetable Pad Thai (p.167)

ACCOMPANIMENTS

Coronation Coleslaw (p.194)

Garlic Parsley Flatbread (p.85)

Garlic Roasted Potatoes with Rosemary (p.212)

Grilled Courgettes with Ginger Crunch (p.210)

Halloumi and Sweet Potato Fries with Chilli Dip (p.86)

Harissa Roasted Chantenay Carrots (p.215)

Hispi Cabbage Noisette (p.207)

Leek and Potato Gratin (p.208)

Roasted Mediterranean Vegetables with Goat's Cheese (p.216)

COLD DESSERTS

Baked Ricotta Cheesecake with Blackberry Coulis (p.273)

Chocolate and Brandy Shots (p.268)

Feathered White Chocolate Cheesecake (p.267)

Glazed French Peach Tart (p.284–6)

Glorious Chocolate Truffle Dessert (p.262–3)

Hazelnut Meringue Roulade (p.261)

Limoncello Passion Panna Cotta (p.270)

Sunrise Fruit Salad (p.283)

Tiramisu Red Fruit Trifle (p.258)

HOT PUDDINGS

Pear and Blueberry Galette (p.278)

Spiced Apple Strudel (p.274)

Sunday Lunch Plum Crumble Cake (p.281)

Windfall Pie (p.277)

SMALL BAKES

Gin and Lime Drizzle Traybake (p.234)

Honeycomb Rocky Road (p.229)

Lemon and Passion Fruit Traybake (p.230)

Posh White Chocolate Shortbread Biscuits (p.252)

Tear and Share Cheese and Herb Rolls (p.255)

The Ultimate Chocolate Brownies (p.220)

Salted Caramel Brownies (p.225)

Star Almond Mince Pies (p.245)

White Chocolate and Pistachio Blondies (p.224)

LARGE CAKES

Banana Fruit Bread (p.246)

Birthday Chocolate Ganache Cake (p.239–41)

Clementine Cake (p.236–8)

Easter Simnel Cake (p.248–9)

Ginger and Orange Polenta Cake (p.226)

Shirl's Fruit Cake (p.242)

Salted Caramel Cake (p.233)

A

almonds
  ginger and orange polenta cake 226
  glorious chocolate truffle dessert 262–3
  posh white chocolate shortbread biscuits 252
  star almond mince pies 245
American-style pancakes with bacon and maple syrup 47
apples
  double mustard chicken 124
  jumbo sausage rolls 88
  spiced apple strudel 274
  windfall pie 277
apricots
  banana fruit bread 246
  Easter simnel cake 248–9
asparagus
  forest bean salad 200
  Greek salad with asparagus 196
  hot-smoked salmon rice and asparagus salad 103
  smashed avocado, asparagus and fried egg on sourdough 45
  smoked salmon and burrata sharing platter 66
aubergines
  Majorcan-style one pot vegetables 188
  roasted Mediterranean veg with goat's cheese 216
  sabzi vegetable curry 184
avocados
  avocado, beetroot and prawn stack 26
  avocado, olive and tomato blinis 24
  chicken, avocado and mango lettuce wraps 57
  eggy bread avocado and ham sandwich 50
  smashed avocado, asparagus and fried egg on sourdough 45
  toasted brioche with avocado, spinach and bacon 52

B

bacon
  American-style pancakes with bacon and maple syrup 47

bacon and egg breakfast croustades 38
beef bourguignon pie 153–4
toasted brioche with avocado, spinach and bacon 52
baked beans: chipchip cassoulet 147
baking 218–55
  banana fruit bread 246
  birthday chocolate ganache cake 239–41
  clementine cake 236–8
  Easter simnel cake 248–9
  gin and lime drizzle traybake 234
  ginger and orange polenta cake 226
  honeycomb rocky road 229
  lemon and passion fruit traybake 230
  posh white chocolate shortbread biscuits 252
  salted caramel brownies 225
  salted caramel cake 233
  Shirl's fruit cake 242
  star almond mince pies 245
  tear and share cheese and herb rolls 255
  the ultimate chocolate brownies 220
  white chocolate and pistachio blondies 224
banana fruit bread 246
basil
  basil olive dip 63
  five veg pasta 178
  herb lemon dressing 200
  Provence tomato and garlic pistou tart 170–1
  roasted tomato and basil soup 34
  smoked salmon and burrata sharing platter 66
  summer soup – pea, potato and basil 28

bean sprouts: vegetable pad Thai 167
beans
  bresaola sharing board with rocket, Parmesan and bean salad 64

chipchip cassoulet 147
  spicy pork with sweet potato and black-eyed beans 148
beef
  beef bourguignon pie 153–4
  beef kofta with tomato salsa 74
  black bean beef noodle stir-fry 157
  bresaola sharing board with rocket, Parmesan and bean salad 64
  fillet steak for two with green peppercorn and brandy sauce 162
  spiced beef with chicory 76
  sticky short beef ribs and lemon coleslaw 158–9
beetroot: avocado, beetroot and prawn stack 26
birthday chocolate ganache cake 239–41
Biscoff biscuits: salted caramel brownies 225
black bean sauce
  black bean beef noodle stir-fry 157
  black bean chicken skewers 69
black-eyed beans, spicy pork with sweet potato and 148
blackberries: baked ricotta cheesecake with blackberry coulis 273
blinis
  avocado, olive and tomato 24
  ginger and chilli prawn 24
  herb blinis 23
  pea and feta 24
blondies, white chocolate and pistachio 224
blue cheese: celery, blue cheese and sage risotto 168
blueberries: pear and blueberry galette 278
brandy
  chocolate and brandy shots 268
  double mustard chicken 124
  green peppercorn and brandy sauce 162
  hazelnut meringue roulade with brandy cream 261
  tiramisu red fruit trifle 258

bread
  bacon and egg breakfast croustades 38
  eggy bread avocado and ham sandwich 50
  garlic parsley flatbread 85
  match day hot dogs 54
  smashed avocado, asparagus and fried egg on sourdough 45
  tear and share cheese and herb rolls 255
  toasted brioche with avocado, spinach and bacon 52
bresaola sharing board with rocket, Parmesan and bean salad 64
Brie: Provence tomato and garlic pistou tart 170–1
brioche: toasted brioche with avocado, spinach and bacon 52
broad beans
  forest bean salad with herb lemon dressing 200
  summer soup – pea, potato and basil 28
broccoli
  broccoli and quinoa salad with feta and yoghurt dressing 204
  summer soup – pea, potato and basil 28
brownies
  salted caramel brownies 225
  the ultimate chocolate brownies 220
brunch 10, 36–59
  American-style pancakes with bacon and maple syrup 47
  bacon and egg breakfast croustades 38
  chicken, avocado and mango lettuce wraps 57
  cinnamon crêpes 49
  eggy bread avocado and ham sandwich 50
  frittata with spinach, feta and tomatoes 42
  fruit kebabs with lemon dip 58
  match day hot dogs 54
  shakshuka 41
  smashed avocado, asparagus and fried egg on sourdough 45
  toasted brioche with avocado,

  spinach and bacon 52
burrata: smoked salmon and burrata sharing platter 66
butternut squash
  curried squash and paneer filo samosas 183
  harissa halloumi and squash skewers 68

C
cabbage
  coronation coleslaw 195
  Hispi cabbage noisette 207
  lemon coleslaw 158–9
  roast chicken breast with creamy mushrooms and cabbage 117
cakes
  birthday chocolate ganache cake 239–41
  clementine cake 236–8
  Easter simnel cake 248–9
  gin and lime drizzle traybake 234
  ginger and orange polenta cake 226
  glorious chocolate truffle dessert 262–3
  lemon and passion fruit traybake 230
  salted caramel cake 233
  Shirl's fruit cake 242
  Sunday lunch plum crumble cake 281
canapés
  herb blinis 23–4
  red pepper, cheese and chive canapé tarts 19
  salmon, goat's cheese and cucumber canapé 17
caramel
  caramelised chestnuts 32
  salted caramel brownies 225
  salted caramel cake 233
carrots
  Coronation coleslaw 195
  duck breast with stir-fry veg and cashew sauce 134
  harissa roasted Chantenay carrots 215
  lemon coleslaw 158–9
  noodle nori salad 199

sabzi vegetable curry 184
shepherd's puff pastry pie 138
Sunday best minted lamb 145
vegetable pad Thai 167
cashew nuts
  duck breast with stir-fry vegetables and cashew sauce 134
  spaghetti with peas and pesto 177
cassoulet, chipchip 147
cauliflower
  cauliflower potato cakes with Parmesan sauce 191
  coriander roasted vegetables with basil olive dip 63
celeriac
  Coronation coleslaw 195
  roast rack of lamb with celeriac purée 142
  smoked haddock and celeriac and potato mash fish pie 104
celery
  celery, blue cheese and sage risotto 168
  coriander roasted vegetables with basil olive dip 63
  Coronation coleslaw 195
ceviche: tuna ceviche with pickled ginger and salsa 79
cheese
  bacon and egg breakfast croustades 38
  basil olive dip 63
  bresaola sharing board with rocket, Parmesan and bean salad 64
  broccoli and quinoa salad with feta and yoghurt dressing 204
  cauliflower potato cakes with Parmesan sauce 191
  celery, blue cheese and sage risotto 168
  chicken, spinach and tomato lasagne 129–31
  eggy bread avocado and ham sandwich 50
  five veg pasta 178
  frittata with spinach, feta and tomatoes 42
  gardener's stuffed squash 180
  garlic parsley flatbread 85

Greek salad 196
halloumi and sweet potato fries with chilli dip 86
harissa halloumi and squash skewers 68
jumbo lentil rolls 91
leek and potato gratin 208
pea and feta blinis 24
porcini, wild mushroom and watercress gratin 174
Provence tomato and garlic pistou tart 170–1
red pepper, cheese and chive canapé tarts 19
roasted Mediterranean veg with goat's cheese 216
smoked haddock and celeriac and potato mash fish pie 104
smoked haddock macaroni cheese 94
smoked salmon and burrata sharing platter 66
spaghetti with peas and pesto 177
tear and share cheese and herb rolls 255
cheesecake
  baked ricotta cheesecake with blackberry coulis 273
  feathered white chocolate cheesecake 267
chestnuts, winter parsnip and chestnut soup with caramelised 32
chia seeds: forest bean salad 200
chicken
  black bean chicken skewers 69
  chicken and spinach herb parcel 126–8
  chicken, avocado and mango lettuce wraps 57
  chicken, spinach and tomato lasagne 129–31
  double mustard chicken 124
  roast chicken breast with creamy mushrooms and cabbage 117
  roasting tin spiced chicken 114
  Thai green curry 123
  Tuscan chicken 133
  two roast chickens with scalloped potatoes 118–19

chickpeas: lamb and chickpea spiced stew 141
chicory, spiced beef with 76
chillies
  chilli dip 86
  chipchip cassoulet 147
  ginger and chilli prawn blinis 24
  prawn stir-fry with ginger, coconut and chilli 108
  shakshuka 41
  spiced tomato relish 54
Chinese five spice: roasting tin spiced chicken 114
chipchip cassoulet 147
chipotle paste
  chipchip cassoulet 147
  spiced tomato relish 54
chives
  cauliflower potato cakes with Parmesan sauce 191
  herb blinis 23
  red pepper, cheese and chive canapé tarts 19
chocolate
  birthday chocolate ganache cake 239–41
  chocolate and brandy shots 268
  feathered white chocolate cheesecake 267
  glorious chocolate truffle dessert 262–3
  honeycomb rocky road 229
  posh white chocolate shortbread biscuits 252
  salted caramel brownies 225
  tiramisu red fruit trifle 258
  the ultimate chocolate brownies 220
  white chocolate and pistachio blondies 224
chutney: eggy bread avocado and ham sandwich 50
cinnamon crêpes 49
clementine cake 236–8
coconut cream: prawn stir-fry with ginger, coconut and chilli 108
coconut milk: Thai green curry 123
coffee: tiramisu red fruit trifle 258

coleslaw
  Coronation coleslaw 195
  sticky short beef ribs and lemon coleslaw 158–9
conversion charts 288–9
cook's notes 13
coriander
  coriander roasted vegetables with basil olive dip 63
  salsa 79
  spiced beef with chicory 76
  vegetable pad Thai 167
Coronation coleslaw 195
coulis, blackberry 273
courgettes
  duck breast with stir-fry veg and cashew sauce 134
  five veg pasta 178
  gardener's stuffed squash 180
  grilled courgettes with ginger crunch 210
  honey-glazed salmon and courgette skewers 72
  prawn stir-fry with ginger, coconut and chilli 108
  roasted Mediterranean veg with goat's cheese 216
crab: hoso maki 81
cream
  birthday chocolate ganache cake 239–41
  chocolate and brandy shots 268
  double mustard chicken 124
  feathered white chocolate cheesecake 267
  glorious chocolate truffle dessert 262–3
  green peppercorn and brandy sauce 162
  hazelnut meringue roulade with brandy cream 261
  lemon and passion fruit traybake 230
  limoncello passion panna cotta 270
  moules marinière 107
  roast chicken breast with creamy mushrooms and cabbage 117
  scallops with garlic king oyster mushrooms and tarragon 110
  tiramisu red fruit trifle 258

Tuscan chicken 133

cream cheese
baked ricotta cheesecake 273
chicken and spinach herb parcel 126–8
ginger and chilli prawn blinis 24
salmon en croute with spinach and dill 98–9
smoked salmon and watercress pâté 20–2
toasted brioche with avocado, spinach and bacon 52

crème fraîche
cauliflower potato cakes with Parmesan sauce 191
chicken, avocado and mango lettuce wraps 57
chicken, spinach and tomato lasagne 129–31
chilli dip 86
herb sauce 98–9
roast rack of lamb with celeriac purée 142

crème patissiere: glazed French peach tart 284–6

crêpes and pancakes
American-style pancakes with bacon and maple syrup 47
cinnamon crêpes 49

croustades, bacon and egg breakfast 38

crumble cake, Sunday lunch plum 281

cucumber
avocado, beetroot and prawn stack 26
cucumber dip 73
Greek salad with asparagus 196
hoso maki 81
salmon, goat's cheese and cucumber canapé 17
smoked salmon and burrata sharing platter 66

curry
Coronation coleslaw 195
curried squash and paneer filo samosas 183
sabzi vegetable curry 184
Thai green curry 123

D

daikon: noodle nori salad 199

desserts and puddings 256–87

digestive biscuits
baked ricotta cheesecake with blackberry coulis 273
feathered white chocolate cheesecake 267
honeycomb rocky road 229

dill
avocado, beetroot and prawn stack 26
hot-smoked salmon rice and asparagus salad 103
salmon, goat's cheese and cucumber canapé 17
salmon en croute with spinach and dill 98–9
smoked salmon and watercress pâté 20–2

dips
basil olive dip 63
chilli dip 86
cucumber dip 73
lemon dip 58

dressings
herb lemon dressing 200
lemon dressing 103
yoghurt dressing 204

duck breast with stir-fry vegetables and cashew sauce 134

E

Easter simnel cake 248–9

eggs 13
bacon and egg breakfast croustades 38
eggy bread avocado and ham sandwich 50
frittata with spinach, feta and tomatoes 42
glazed French peach tart 284–6
glorious chocolate truffle dessert 262–3
hazelnut meringue roulade with brandy cream 261
hot-smoked salmon rice and asparagus salad 103
shakshuka 41
smashed avocado, asparagus and fried egg on sourdough 45

smoked haddock and celeriac and potato mash fish pie 104

F

feathered white chocolate cheesecake 267

fennel: roasting tin spiced chicken 114

feta
broccoli and quinoa salad with feta and yoghurt dressing 204
frittata with spinach, feta and tomatoes 42
gardener's stuffed squash 180
Greek salad with asparagus 196
pea and feta blinis 24

filo pastry
curried squash and paneer filo samosas 183
spiced apple strudel 274

first courses 14–35
autumn leek and mushroom soup 31
avocado, beetroot and prawn stack 26
herb blinis 23–4
red pepper, cheese and chive canapé tarts 19
roasted tomato and basil soup 34
salmon, goat's cheese and cucumber canapé 17
smoked salmon and watercress pâté 20–2
summer soup – pea, potato and basil 28
winter parsnip and chestnut soup with caramelised chestnuts 32

fish 13, 92–111
honey-glazed salmon and courgette skewers 72
hot-smoked salmon rice and asparagus salad 103
miso salmon with aromatic spinach 97
salmon, goat's cheese and cucumber canapé 17
salmon en croute with spinach and dill 98–9
smoked haddock and celeriac and potato mash fish pie 104

smoked haddock macaroni cheese 94

smoked salmon and burrata sharing platter 66

smoked salmon and watercress pâté 20–2

sushi squares with smoked salmon and pickled ginger 83

tuna ceviche with pickled ginger and salsa 79

five veg pasta 178

flatbread, garlic parsley 85

forest bean salad with herb lemon dressing 200

French peach tart, glazed 284–6

fries: halloumi and sweet potato fries with chilli dip 86

frittata with spinach, feta and tomatoes 42

fruit

fruit kebabs with lemon dip 58

sunrise fruit salad 283

tiramisu red fruit trifle 258

see also individual types of fruit

fruit bread, banana 246

fruit cake, Shirl's 242

G

galette, pear and blueberry 278

ganache icing 239–41

garam masala

chicken, avocado and mango lettuce wraps 57

curried squash and paneer filo samosas 183

sabzi vegetable curry 184

gardener's stuffed squash 180

garlic

garlic parsley flatbread 85

garlic roasted potatoes with rosemary 212

moules marinière 107

Provence tomato and garlic pistou tart 170–1

scallops with garlic king oyster mushrooms and tarragon 110

two roast chickens with scalloped potatoes 118–19

gin and lime drizzle traybake 234

ginger

Easter simnel cake 248–9

ginger and chilli prawn blinis 24

ginger and orange polenta cake 226

grilled courgettes with ginger crunch 210

noodle nori salad 199

prawn stir-fry with ginger, coconut and chilli 108

sushi squares with smoked salmon and pickled ginger 83

tuna ceviche with pickled ginger and salsa 79

glacé cherries: Easter simnel cake 248–9

glazed French peach tart 284–6

glorious chocolate truffle dessert 262–3

goat's cheese

jumbo lentil rolls 91

roasted Mediterranean veg with goat's cheese 216

salmon, goat's cheese and cucumber canapé 17

gratins

leek and potato gratin 208

porcini, wild mushroom and watercress gratin 174

gravy, white wine 151–2

Greek salad with asparagus 196

green beans

forest bean salad with herb lemon dressing 200

Thai green curry 123

green curry, Thai 123

Gruyère

leek and potato gratin 208

smoked haddock and celeriac and potato mash fish pie 104

H

haddock

smoked haddock and celeriac and potato mash fish pie 104

smoked haddock macaroni cheese 94

halloumi

halloumi and sweet potato fries with chilli dip 86

harissa halloumi and squash skewers 68

ham: eggy bread avocado and ham sandwich 50

harissa

beef kofta with tomato salsa 74

harissa halloumi and squash skewers 68

harissa roasted Chantenay carrots 215

hazelnut meringue roulade with brandy cream 261

herbs

chicken and spinach herb parcel 126–8

chicken, spinach and tomato lasagne 129–31

herb blinis 23

herb lemon dressing 200

herb sauce 98–9

tear and share cheese and herb rolls 255

Hispi cabbage

Hispi cabbage noisette 207

roast chicken breast with creamy mushrooms and cabbage 117

hoi sin sauce: spiced beef with chicory 76

honey-glazed salmon and courgette skewers 72

honeycomb rocky road 229

horseradish sauce

avocado, beetroot and prawn stack 26

smoked salmon and watercress pâté 20–2

hoso maki 81

hot dogs, match day 54

hot-smoked salmon rice and asparagus salad 103

J

jumbo lentil rolls 91

jumbo sausage rolls 88

K

kale: porcini, wild mushroom and watercress gratin 174

kebabs

fruit kebabs with lemon dip 58

see also skewers

king oyster mushrooms: scallops with garlic king oyster mushrooms and tarragon 110

koftas
  beef kofta with tomato salsa 74
  minted lamb kofta with
  cucumber dip 73

L
lamb
  lamb and chickpea spiced stew
  141
  minted lamb kofta with
  cucumber dip 73
  roast rack of lamb with
  celeriac purée 142
  shepherd's puff pastry pie 138
  Sunday best minted lamb 145
lasagne, chicken, spinach and
  tomato 129–31
leeks
  autumn leek and mushroom
  soup 31
  leek and potato gratin 208
  Sunday best minted lamb 145
lemon curd
  lemon dip 58
  limoncello passion panna cotta
  270
lemons
  herb lemon dressing 200
  lemon and passion fruit
  traybake 230
  lemon dressing 103
  limoncello passion panna cotta
  270
  sticky short beef ribs and
  lemon coleslaw 158–9
lentils: jumbo lentil rolls 91
lettuce
  broccoli and quinoa salad with
  feta and yoghurt dressing 204
  chicken, avocado and mango
  lettuce wraps 57
limes
  gin and lime drizzle traybake
  234
  tuna ceviche with pickled
  ginger and salsa 79
limoncello passion panna cotta
  270

M
macaroni cheese, smoked
  haddock 94
Majorcan-style one pot

vegetables 188
mango
  chicken, avocado and mango
  lettuce wraps 57
  fruit kebabs with lemon dip 58
  sunrise fruit salad 283
mango chutney
  Coronation coleslaw 195
  sabzi vegetable curry 184
  toasted brioche with avocado,
  spinach and bacon 52
maple syrup
  American-style pancakes with
  bacon and maple syrup 47
  sticky short beef ribs and
  lemon coleslaw 158–9
marmalade: clementine cake
  236–8
marzipan
  Easter simnel cake 248–9
  star almond mince pies 245
mascarpone cheese
  chocolate and brandy shots 268
  feathered white chocolate
  cheesecake 267
  tiramisu red fruit trifle 258
match day hot dogs 54
mayonnaise
  chicken, avocado and mango
  lettuce wraps 57
  Coronation coleslaw 195
  lemon coleslaw 158–9
meat 13
  see also beef; lamb; pork
melon: sunrise fruit salad 283
menus 10–12
meringues: hazelnut meringue
  roulade with brandy cream
  261
mince pies, star almond 245
mint
  herb lemon dressing 200
  jumbo lentil rolls 91
  lemon dip 58
  minted lamb kofta with
  cucumber dip 73
  Provence tomato and garlic
  pistou tart 170–1
  Sunday best minted lamb 145
  yoghurt dressing 204
miso salmon with aromatic

spinach 97
moules marinière 107
mousse: chocolate and brandy
  shots 268
mushrooms
  autumn leek and mushroom
  soup 31
  bacon and egg breakfast
  croustades 38
  beef bourguignon pie 153–4
  black bean beef noodle stir-fry
  157
  celery, blue cheese and sage
  risotto 168
  chicken, spinach and tomato
  lasagne 129–31
  five veg pasta 178
  gardener's stuffed squash 180
  porcini, wild mushroom and
  watercress gratin 174
  roast chicken breast with
  creamy mushrooms and
  cabbage 117
  scallops with garlic king oyster
  mushrooms and tarragon 110
  shepherd's puff pastry pie 138
  Sunday best minted lamb 145
  Thai green curry 123
mussels: moules marinière 107
mustard
  double mustard chicken 124
  green peppercorn and brandy
  sauce 162

N
noodles
  black bean beef noodle stir-fry
  157
  noodle nori salad 199
  vegetable pad Thai 167
nori
  hoso maki 81
  noodle nori salad 199

O
oats: Sunday lunch plum
  crumble cake 281
olives
  avocado, olive and tomato
  blinis 24
  basil olive dip 63

bresaola sharing board with rocket, Parmesan and bean salad 64
  Greek salad with asparagus 196
onions: shepherd's puff pastry pie 138
orange juice
  Shirl's fruit cake 242
  sunrise fruit salad 283
oranges: ginger and orange polenta cake 226

P
pad Thai, vegetable 167
pancakes and crêpes
  American-style pancakes with bacon and maple syrup 47
  cinnamon crêpes 49
paneer: curried squash and paneer filo samosas 183
panna cotta, limoncello passion 270
papaya: sunrise fruit salad 283
paprika: lamb and chickpea spiced stew 141
Parmesan
  basil olive dip 63
  bresaola sharing board 64
  cauliflower potato cakes with Parmesan sauce 191
  five veg pasta 178
  gardener's stuffed squash 180
  porcini, wild mushroom and watercress gratin 174
  Provence tomato and garlic pistou tart 170–1
  red pepper, cheese and chive canapé tarts 19
  spaghetti with peas and pesto 177
parsley
  garlic parsley flatbread 85
  hot-smoked salmon rice and asparagus salad 103
parsnips: winter parsnip and chestnut soup with caramelised chestnuts 32
passion fruit
  limoncello passion panna cotta 270
  sunrise fruit salad 283

passion fruit curd: lemon and passion fruit traybake 230
pasta
  chicken, spinach and tomato lasagne 129–31
  five veg pasta 178
  smoked haddock macaroni cheese 94
  spaghetti with peas and pesto 177
pâté, smoked salmon and watercress 20–2
pea shoots: tuna ceviche with pickled ginger and salsa 79
peaches: glazed French peach tart 284–6
peanuts: vegetable pad Thai 167
pear and blueberry galette 278
peas
  celery, blue cheese and sage risotto 168
  pea and feta blinis 24
  sabzi vegetable curry 184
  smoked haddock macaroni cheese 94
  spaghetti with peas and pesto 177
  summer soup – pea, potato and basil 28
peppercorns: green peppercorn and brandy sauce 162
peppers
  black bean beef noodle stir-fry 157
  chipchip cassoulet 147
  coriander roasted vegetables with basil olive dip 63
  duck breast with stir-fry veg and cashew sauce 134
  five veg pasta 178
  frittata with spinach, feta and tomatoes 42
  harissa halloumi and squash skewers 68
  Majorcan-style one pot vegetables 188
  noodle nori salad 199
  red pepper, cheese and chive canapé tarts 19
  roasted Mediterranean veg with goat's cheese 216
  roasting tin spiced chicken 114

sabzi vegetable curry 184
salmon en croute with spinach and dill 98–9
spiced tomato relish 54
spicy pork with sweet potato and black-eyed beans 148
Tuscan chicken 133
vegetable pad Thai 167
pesto, spaghetti with peas and 177
petits pois
  celery, blue cheese and sage risotto 168
  pea and feta blinis 24
  sabzi vegetable curry 184
  smoked haddock macaroni cheese 94
  spaghetti with peas and pesto 177
  summer soup – pea, potato and basil 28
pickle: eggy bread avocado and ham sandwich 50
pies
  beef bourguignon pie 153–4
  shepherd's puff pastry pie 138
  smoked haddock and celeriac and potato mash fish pie 104
  star almond mince pies 245
  windfall pie 277
pineapple: fruit kebabs with lemon dip 58
pistachios
  beef kofta with tomato salsa 74
  white chocolate and pistachio blondies 224
pistou: Provence tomato and garlic pistou tart 170–1
plums: Sunday lunch plum crumble cake 281
polenta: ginger and orange polenta cake 226
pomegranate: sunrise fruit salad 283
porcini, wild mushroom and watercress gratin 174
pork
  loin of stuffed pork with crackling and white wine gravy 151–2
  spicy pork with sweet potato and black-eyed beans 148

posh white chocolate shortbread
  biscuits 252
potatoes
  autumn leek and mushroom
    soup 31
  cauliflower potato cakes with
    Parmesan sauce 191
  garlic roasted potatoes with
    rosemary 212
  leek and potato gratin 208
  Majorcan-style one pot
    vegetables 188
  sabzi vegetable curry 184
  smoked haddock and celeriac
    and potato mash fish pie 104
  summer soup – pea, potato
    and basil 28
  two roast chickens with
    scalloped potatoes 118–19
poultry 112–35
  see also chicken; duck
prawns
  avocado, beetroot and prawn
    stack 26
  ginger and chilli prawn blinis
    24
  prawn stir-fry with ginger,
    coconut and chilli 108
Provence tomato and garlic
  pistou tart 170–1
puddings and desserts 256–87
puff pastry
  beef bourguignon pie 153–4
  chicken and spinach herb
    parcel 126–8
  jumbo lentil rolls 91
  jumbo sausage rolls 88
  salmon en croute with spinach
    and dill 98–9
  shepherd's puff pastry pie 138
pumpkin seeds
  broccoli and quinoa salad with
    feta and yoghurt dressing 204
  forest bean salad with herb
    lemon dressing 200
Puy lentils: jumbo lentil rolls 91

Q
quinoa: broccoli and quinoa
  salad with feta and yoghurt
  dressing 204

R
radishes: pea and feta blinis 24
raspberries: hazelnut meringue
  roulade 261
relish, spiced tomato 54
rhubarb: windfall pie 277
rice
  celery, blue cheese and sage
    risotto 168
  hoso maki 81
  hot-smoked salmon rice and
    asparagus salad 103
  simple sushi rice 80
  sushi squares with smoked
    salmon and pickled ginger 83
ricotta
  baked ricotta cheesecake with
    blackberry coulis 273
risotto, celery, blue cheese and
  sage 168
rocket: bresaola sharing board
  with rocket, Parmesan and
  bean salad 64
rocky road, honeycomb 229
rolls, tear and share cheese and
  herb 255
rosemary, garlic roasted
  potatoes with 212
roulades: hazelnut meringue
  roulade with brandy cream
  261
runner beans: forest bean salad
  with herb lemon dressing 200

S
sabzi vegetable curry 184
salads
  bresaola sharing board with
    rocket, Parmesan and bean
    salad 64
  broccoli and quinoa salad with
    feta and yoghurt dressing 204
  Coronation coleslaw 195
  forest bean salad with herb
    lemon dressing 200
  Greek salad with asparagus 196
  hot-smoked salmon rice and
    asparagus salad 103
  lemon coleslaw 158–9
  noodle nori salad 199
  sunrise fruit salad 283
salmon

honey-glazed salmon and
  courgette skewers 72
hot-smoked salmon rice and
  asparagus salad 103
miso salmon with aromatic
  spinach 97
salmon, goat's cheese and
  cucumber canapé 17
salmon en croute with spinach
  and dill 98–9
smoked salmon and burrata
  sharing platter 66
smoked salmon and watercress
  pâté 20–2
sushi squares with smoked
  salmon and pickled ginger 83
salsa
  tomato salsa 74
  tuna ceviche with pickled
    ginger and salsa 79
salted caramel
  salted caramel brownies 225
  salted caramel cake 233
samosas, curried squash and
  paneer filo 183
sandwiches, eggy bread avocado
  and ham 50
sauces
  herb sauce 98–9
  white wine gravy 151–2
sausages
  chipchip cassoulet 147
  jumbo sausage rolls 88
  loin of stuffed pork with
    crackling and white wine
    gravy 151–2
  match day hot dogs 54
scallops with garlic king oyster
  mushrooms and tarragon 110
seafood
  moules marinière 107
  prawn stir-fry with ginger,
    coconut and chilli 108
  scallops with garlic king oyster
    mushrooms and tarragon 110
shakshuka 41
shallots: beef bourguignon pie
  153–4
sharing 11, 60–91
  beef kofta with tomato salsa 74
  black bean chicken skewers 69
  bresaola sharing board with

rocket, Parmesan and bean salad 64

coriander roasted vegetables with basil olive dip 63

garlic parsley flatbread 85

halloumi and sweet potato fries with chilli dip 86

harissa halloumi and squash skewers 68

honey-glazed salmon and courgette skewers 72

hoso maki 81

jumbo lentil rolls 91

jumbo sausage rolls 88

minted lamb kofta with cucumber dip 73

simple sushi rice 80

smoked salmon and burrata sharing platter 66

spiced beef with chicory 76

sushi squares with smoked salmon and pickled ginger 83

tuna ceviche with pickled ginger and salsa 79

shepherd's puff pastry pie 138

Shirl's fruit cake 242

shortbread biscuits, posh white chocolate 252

simnel cake, Easter 248–9

skewers

black bean chicken skewers 69

harissa halloumi and squash skewers 68

honey-glazed salmon and courgette skewers 72

smashed avocado, asparagus and fried egg on sourdough 45

smoked haddock

smoked haddock and celeriac and potato mash fish pie 104

smoked haddock macaroni cheese 94

smoked salmon

hot-smoked salmon rice and asparagus salad 103

salmon, goat's cheese and cucumber canapé 17

smoked salmon and burrata sharing platter 66

smoked salmon and watercress pâté 20–2

sushi squares with smoked

salmon and pickled ginger 83

soups

autumn leek and mushroom 31

pea, potato and basil 28

roasted tomato and basil 34

winter parsnip and chestnut with caramelised chestnuts 32

sourdough, smashed avocado, asparagus and fried egg on 45

soured cream

baked ricotta cheesecake with blackberry coulis 273

Coronation coleslaw 195

spaghetti with peas and pesto 177

spiced apple strudel 274

spiced beef with chicory 76

spicy pork with sweet potato and black-eyed beans 148

spinach

chicken and spinach herb parcel 126–8

chicken, spinach and tomato lasagne 129–31

frittata with spinach, feta and tomatoes 42

miso salmon with aromatic spinach 97

prawn stir-fry with ginger, coconut and chilli 108

salmon en croute with spinach and dill 98–9

smoked haddock and celeriac and potato mash fish pie 104

toasted brioche with avocado, spinach and bacon 52

Tuscan chicken 133

sponges, trifle: tiramisu red fruit trifle 258

spring onions

black bean beef noodle stir-fry 157

cauliflower potato cakes with Parmesan sauce 191

duck breast with stir-fry vegetables and cashew sauce 134

hot-smoked salmon rice and asparagus salad 103

squash

curried squash and paneer filo samosas 183

gardener's stuffed squash 180

harissa halloumi and squash skewers 68

star almond mince pies 245

stews

chipchip cassoulet 147

lamb and chickpea spiced stew 141

Sunday best minted lamb 145

sticky short beef ribs and lemon coleslaw 158–9

stir-fries

black bean beef noodle stir-fry 157

duck breast with stir-fry vegetables and cashew sauce 134

prawn stir-fry with ginger, coconut and chilli 108

strawberries: fruit kebabs with lemon dip 58

strudel, spiced apple 274

sugar snap peas: five veg pasta 178

sultanas

banana fruit bread 246

Easter simnel cake 248–9

Shirl's fruit cake 242

summer soup – pea, potato and basil 28

Sunday best minted lamb 145

Sunday lunch plum crumble cake 281

sunrise fruit salad 283

sushi 80

hoso maki 81

sushi squares with smoked salmon and pickled ginger 83

sweet potatoes

halloumi and sweet potato fries with chilli dip 86

roasting tin spiced chicken 114

spicy pork with sweet potato and black-eyed beans 148

T

tarragon, scallops with garlic king oyster mushrooms and 110

tarts

glazed French peach tart 284–6

Provence tomato and garlic

pistou tart 170–1
red pepper, cheese and chive canapé tarts 19
tear and share cheese and herb rolls 255
tenderstem broccoli and quinoa salad with feta and yoghurt dressing 204
Thai green curry 123
tiramisu red fruit trifle 258
tomatoes
  avocado, olive and tomato blinis 24
  chicken, spinach and tomato lasagne 129–31
  chipchip cassoulet 147
  frittata with spinach, feta and tomatoes 42
  gardener's stuffed squash 180
  Greek salad with asparagus 196
  honey-glazed salmon and courgette skewers 72
  jumbo lentil rolls 91
  lamb and chickpea spiced stew 141
  Majorcan-style one pot vegetables 188
  Provence tomato and garlic pistou tart 170–1
  red pepper, cheese and chive canapé tarts 19
  roasted tomato and basil soup 34
  sabzi vegetable curry 184
  salsa 79
  shakshuka 41
  smoked salmon and burrata sharing platter 66
  spiced tomato relish 54
  spicy pork with sweet potato and black-eyed beans 148
  toasted brioche with avocado, spinach and bacon 52
  tomato salsa 74
  Tuscan chicken 133
traybakes
  gin and lime drizzle traybake 234
  lemon and passion fruit traybake 230
trifle, tiramisu red fruit 258
truffles: glorious chocolate truffle

dessert 262–3
tuna ceviche with pickled ginger and salsa 79
Tuscan chicken 133

U
the ultimate chocolate brownies 220

V
vegetables
  coriander roasted vegetables with basil olive dip 63
  duck breast with stir-fry vegetables and cashew sauce 134
  five veg pasta 178
  Majorcan-style one pot vegetables 188
  roasted Mediterranean veg with goat's cheese 216
  sabzi vegetable curry 184
  vegetable pad Thai 167
  see also individual vegetables
veggie mains 164–91
  cauliflower potato cakes with Parmesan sauce 191
  celery, blue cheese and sage risotto 168
  curried squash and paneer filo samosas 183
  five veg pasta 178
  gardener's stuffed squash 180
  Majorcan-style one pot vegetables 188
  porcini, wild mushroom and watercress gratin 174
  Provence tomato and garlic pistou tart 170–1
  sabzi vegetable curry 184
  spaghetti with peas and pesto 177
  vegetable pad Thai 167

W
wasabi: hoso maki 81
watercress
  porcini, wild mushroom and watercress gratin 174
  smoked salmon and watercress pâté 20–2
white chocolate
  feathered white chocolate

cheesecake 267
posh white chocolate shortbread biscuits 252
white chocolate and pistachio blondies 224
wild mushrooms: porcini, wild mushroom and watercress gratin 174
windfall pie 277
wine
  beef bourguignon pie 153–4
  celery, blue cheese and sage risotto 168
  loin of stuffed pork with crackling and white wine gravy 151–2
  moules marinière 107
  roast chicken breast with creamy mushrooms and cabbage 117
  scallops with garlic king oyster mushrooms and tarragon 110
  shepherd's puff pastry pie 138
  Sunday best minted lamb 145
  Tuscan chicken 133
  two roast chickens with scalloped potatoes 118–19
winter parsnip and chestnut soup with caramelised chestnuts 32
wraps, chicken, avocado and mango lettuce 57

Y
yoghurt
  broccoli and quinoa salad with feta and yoghurt dressing 204
  cucumber dip 73
  lemon dip 58

THANK YOUS

This is one of the most important pages in the book, as it gives me a chance to thank my team for making a new book happen each year! At home we are a team of three in the kitchen – Lucy Young is very much in charge of everything. What can I say about Lucy Young after 32 years working together? Firstly, we think and work as a team, and really have a passion for what we do. Any success that I have achieved is hugely thanks to wonderful Luce. She is one in a million. The days when we are trying out recipes are the fun ones! Lucinda McCord is at the practical helm, taking tremendous care to achieve the best results. She has been with us for 21 years, straight from cookery training, and is the fastest, most efficient cook we know – and one of the loveliest people. And with me, that's the three of us. We are always excited to start a new book. Once the title and format is decided, it's the three of us around the table pooling ideas, thoughts and recipes.

All the recipes are tried and tested throughout the year, until they are just right. And after the final test, we share them with our families for comments, too. Embracing modern technology, we take photos on our phones before everyone dives in for a taste! These photos act as a reminder and a guide for when we're shooting the gorgeous glossy photos for the book.

The skill, time and precision needed for these photos is exceptional. What a special team they are – brilliant photographer Laura Edwards, the very best food stylist Lisa Harrison and the props all styled beautifully by Tabitha Hawkins.

Jo Penfold deserves the hugest thanks for working her magic on my hair and makeup and always making sure I scrub up ok! And Tess Wright, our fun energetic stylist, finds the loveliest clothes for me to wear.

Thank you to Lizzy Gray and Charlotte Macdonald at BBC Books for keeping us on track and to designer Abi Hartshorne and the lovely Jo Roberts-Miller, our very best editor.

Finally, thanks to our agents – the superb Caroline Wood, our Literary Agent at FBA, who guides us through and with Michele Topham removes every ounce of stress, and our Media Agent Joanna Kaye at KBJ Management, our guardian angel who makes things happen with all the love and care, aided by Theia Nankivell; we are very lucky to have the best people around us.

And to you, the readers, thank you for your continued support. You are the most loyal readers and it is for you that I write these recipes and I am ever thankful to be still doing what I love – teaching and sharing a love of cooking.

Mary Berry

Luce and I – always time to laugh.

Lucinda, me and Luce recipe testing.

1

BBC Books, an imprint of Ebury Publishing
20 Vauxhall Bridge Road,
London SW1V 2SA

BBC Books is part of the Penguin Random House group of companies
whose addresses can be found at global.penguinrandomhouse.com

Penguin
Random House
UK

Copyright © Mary Berry 2022

Photography by Laura Edwards

Mary Berry has asserted her right to be identified as the author of this
Work in accordance with the Copyright, Designs and Patents Act 1988

First published by BBC Books in 2022

www.penguin.co.uk

A CIP catalogue record for this book is available from the British Library

ISBN 9781785947902

Publishing Director: Lizzy Gray
Senior Editor: Charlotte Macdonald
Project Editor and Copyeditor: Jo Roberts-Miller
Food Stylist: Lisa Harrison
Prop Stylist: Tabitha Hawkins
Food Stylist Assistant: Jess McIntosh
Design: Hart Studio

Colour origination by Altaimage, London

Printed and bound in Germany by Mohn Media Mohndruck GmbH

Penguin Random House is committed to a sustainable future for
our business, our readers and our planet. This book is made
from Forest Stewardship Council® certified paper.